CHILDREN OF
RESISTANCE

CHILDREN OF RESISTANCE

ON CHILDREN, REPRESSION AND THE LAW IN APARTHEID SOUTH AFRICA

Edited by

Victoria Brittain & Abdul S. Minty

KLIPTOWN BOOKS

LONDON

First published in 1988 by Kliptown Books Ltd,
Canon Collins House, 64 Essex Road, London N1 8LR.

ISBN No. 0 904759 87 3 (Paperback), 0 904759 89 X (Hardback)

Phototypeset in 10pt Melior and
printed in England by A.G. Bishop & Sons Ltd, Orpington, Kent.

CONTENTS

FOREWORD

In this very turbulent world, across the face of the earth there are many struggles for human rights. But I believe that nowhere in the world has this struggle found a clearer focal point than in South Africa. And that focal point has been there ever since the beginning of this century. The Union of South Africa, as it was then called, came into being by the deprivation of the franchise of the African people. One of the founding fathers of the African National Congress, Sol Plaatje, recognised in the Native Land Act of 1913 the reality of apartheid and pleaded with the world community, all those 70 long years ago, to take action. His plea was unheeded.

Again and again in the course of the struggle it has been the children who have themselves recognised that it is their future which apartheid destroys. They have seen its destructiveness against their fellows, and in the life imprisonment of their leaders. They have felt it in their very being, through multiple deprivations and in the break-up of family life.

This basic moral evil can never end until apartheid itself is destroyed, and it was that knowledge which brought the children of Soweto out onto the streets over ten years ago, with no weapons in their hands. The only weapon they had was the moral rightness of their cause. They were met as always by naked force. Children as young as seven years old were shot down for making that protest for their own future. In the last four years since the promulgation of the new constitution in South Africa and since the continuing States of Emergency have been imposed, it has been children who have been a major target of oppression. A state which is prepared to use its military and paramilitary might to destroy children is a state which must be outlawed totally from the world community until its ideological base – apartheid – is destroyed.

Rt. Reverend Bishop Trevor Huddleston C.R, Convenor of the Harare Conference, speaking at the opening ceremony

**Many people have tried to speak for us . . .
We prefer to speak for ourselves.**

A South African activist

A Child's Experience

Moses Madia, aged 12, from Soweto, recounted his experience to a lawyer who put it into the form of an affidavit for use in legal proceedings

On Friday 17 October 1986 at approximately 12h00 I and three of my friends, Charles, Joel and Zachariah, went to buy some cool drinks at the garage. I and my friends often go to this garage as we buy refreshments there and are friendly with the manager. From time to time the manager, whose name is Alec, gives us odd jobs such as the running of errands or the washing of cars. We proceeded to the Supermarket where we bought vetkoek (dough-nuts) and chips for Alec. We did not buy any food for ourselves as we did not have sufficient money.

After we bought the food we walked back to the garage to give the food to Alec. When we were approximately 100 metres from the garage, a white police van came driving down the road. It pulled up next to us and three black policemen climbed out of the front of the van and called us.

I can remember that the driver was the first person to speak and he said to us 'You don't know me, today you are going to know me, my name is Tshabalala'. He then told us to climb into the back of the police van otherwise we would be shot. We were completely amazed at what was taking place and I asked the policeman why he was doing this to us, but received no explanation. The other policeman who was standing next to Tshabalala, an older man who was bald and of average height, told us that if we did not listen to them, they would burn us. Zachariah then asked what we had done to deserve this kind of treatment, but again received no explanation. Tshabalala would not listen to us and ordered us to climb into the back of the van. He then opened the door of the van and the four of us climbed into the back. When we were in the van one of the policemen pointed a handgun at us through the door and told us that he would shoot us just now. When he pointed this handgun at me I was so scared that I could only look at him and was unable to speak.

I noticed that there was another youth in the back of the police van with us. I saw that the area of his buttocks was covered in blood. Zachariah asked him what had happened and he told us that he had been shot by the police and that it was causing him great pain. Zachariah asked him why he had been shot, to which

1

he simply shook his head and did not reply.

We were unable to see out of the van as there were canvas strips on the side of the vehicle. We stopped a short while later at a house in Zone 3 Diepkloof. I was unable to see the number of the house and I am therefore unable to properly describe the house.

After a short while the door of the police van was opened and a youth climbed in. He was unknown to me at the time although I later learned that his name was Rocky. He was approximately 20 years old and was crying when he entered the back of the van. There was blood coming from what appeared to be a deep gash behind his ear. When Charles asked him what had happened he told us that the man we had come to know as Tshabalala had hit him with his gun behind his ear. At this point I knew that all of us in the back of the police van were in some kind of trouble and although I did not know why we were being detained I put my head in my hands and started to cry.

We moved off and after a short while stopped again. After approximately five minutes another youth climbed into the back of the van. He was also unknown to me although I later came to know him as Sammy, as he was to spend some time with us in the police cells at Orlando Police Station.

Joel asked Sammy why he had been arrested, to which he replied that he did not know. When he asked us why we were in the police van we replied that we had been walking back from the shops with vetkoek and chips which we had bought when the police van had stopped next to us and we had been told to climb into the van otherwise we would be shot.

A short while later the police van arrived at Orlando Police Station and we were taken into a room at the police station. The room was fairly bare, with only a chair, a bench and a table in it. As soon as Tshabalala and the other two policemen who had detained us brought us into the room, the two policemen that were present in the room immediately went out and arrived back a short while later accompanied by a number of other policemen. The only policeman whose name I know is Tshabalala.

The policemen were quite silent and were standing around the walls. It was then that I noticed that Tshabalala was holding a long piece of hosepipe which was curved, green and quite thick. All of us who had been arrested and placed in the back of the police van were in this room and because I was the smallest I tried to hide myself by standing behind Charles, in the hope that if Tshabalala began to use the long piece of hosepipe I would in some way receive protection from the larger boys with whom I had been arrested.

2

One of the policemen wrote down our names and addresses. Tshabalala then swung around with the green hosepipe and hit Charles with it across his back. I was standing quite close to Charles and I can remember hearing the blow which plunged Charles forward and he began to scream. Tshabalala seemed to go into a type of frenzy and although Charles begged him to stop, Tshabalala continued to hit out with the green hosepipe so that Charles and all of us received blows from it. As we tried to escape from the green hosepipe we ran into each other, into the walls and occasionally into policemen who would then slap and push us back towards Tshabalala. I was so scared and the pain so extreme that everything seemed to flash before my eyes as I tried to avoid the hosepipe. Most of us were crying and I recall that Tshabalala passed on the hosepipe to other policemen who also used it upon us.

The policemen would hit us in bouts, sometimes lasting a few minutes and longer. During all of this, various policemen would leave the room while others would come in and take part in the assaults upon us. The police asked us no questions and merely shouted at us, calling us 'siyanyova' (troublemakers).

At some stage that afternoon we were told to lie down with our stomachs on the floor. When we had done so those policemen present in the room started to kick and stamp on us with their shoes and boots. As we tried to roll and avoid the blows they would swear and shout at us, telling us not to move otherwise it would be worse for us.

My back and shoulders were so painful from the hosepipe that the blows from the boots merely came as shocks upon my body and did not really add to the pain. I do remember, however, that each time the boot came down upon my back it would force my face into the floor and at times I thought that my skull would break. During my time on the floor, one of the policemen whom I was not able to see, kicked me hard on the left elbow joint and it was extremely painful. I still have difficulty moving this elbow freely and there is swelling and a bump on it which is quite visible.

After a while the assaults came to an end and it was then that I noticed that my friend Charles was unconscious. He had rolled over onto his back and he lay there with his eyes closed and very still.

One of the policemen who were present in the room instructed me and certain of the other detainees to carry Charles out of the room and into the back of the police van which was outside. I and Joel took Charles' legs while Sammy and Zachariah held his

3

shoulders and we carried him to the police van and placed him on the floor in the back. Victor had been told while we were in the room that he should also climb into the back of the police van and he then limped to the van.

Soon after we had put Charles in the back of the van, Tshabalala instructed Zachariah to also climb into the back of the van as he had a deep cut over his eye and there was blood on the side of his face. I was then told to return to the room in which we had been assaulted. Sammy, Rocky, Joel and myself were in the room at this point as were a few policemen. I am unable to describe these particular policemen, however they were all dressed in blue uniforms and appeared to me to be very large men. They instructed us to do exercises. Although we were unsure as to what exercises we should do, the policemen demonstrated a type of push-up which was done with clenched fists on the floor. We had to push up with our hands and jump so that one landed on your fists on the downward motion of the push-up.

I am unsure as to how long these exercises continued except to say that they stopped approximately 10 to 15 minutes before the return of Zachariah, Charles and Victor, who had been taken to hospital. They were brought back into the room and told to sit with us in the room. Victor was unable to sit, and lay on the one side of his body.

Thereafter we were all taken into another room where a black policeman in a blue uniform took down our names and addresses. In this room were also two women and a small boy. One of the policemen said to the small boy that he should point out, with reference to the seven of us, which of us had been 'there'. The small boy pointed at Victor and said that he was there and that he had had a petrol bomb. At this point the two women who were in the room pointed to the rest of us and said that we had not been 'there' and that we should be taken home to which the policeman replied that we could not be taken home. I had never seen these two women or this small boy who pointed out Victor, before, and I deny that I was part of any incident in which petrol bombs or any violence was involved.

We were led out of the room and placed together in one cell. When we got into the cell, I tried to lie down as I was in a lot of pain. However, my back was too sore for me to lie on it and I consequently lay on my side. A short while later, soon after it had become dark, two black policemen came into our cell. The one was short, squatly built, with short hair and was approximately 30 years of age. I can remember that his head seemed to me to be pointed. The other policeman who had come into the cell was the

4

same one who had locked us into the cell earlier. He carried a bunch of keys and was dressed in a plain navy blue blazer. He was approximately 22 years old and stood to the one side of the cell while the short squat policeman started to approach us. The squat policeman was carrying what appeared to be the same green hosepipe that we had been thrashed with earlier.

I tried to back away from him against the wall of the cell and I was relieved when he stopped and asked us for our names and addresses which he then wrote down. I thought that this was to be the end of the assaults and that he would leave. However, he then advanced upon us and lashed out with the green hosepipe. I realised that we were about to go through what we had gone through earlier that afternoon and I started to scream in the hope that someone, somewhere, in the police station would come to our assistance and stop the assaults.

This policeman continued to lash out at us, kick us, hit us and shout and swear for some time. During this period I remember that I crouched up against the wall with my head between my knees, at which point the policeman in coming past me kicked me just below the knee on my left leg. The pain was so severe that I felt it shoot up my leg and down to my toes. I rolled over screaming and tried to bury my head in the point where the wall meets the floor, hoping that the policeman would take pity on me and leave me alone.

The short squat policeman did lay off me for a short while but some time later I heard my name being shouted by him. When I looked around he pointed at me and shouted for me to come to him. I slowly climbed to my feet and walked towards him. I was so scared that I was unable to speak. As I got close to him, he punched me hard in my stomach. The blow smashed me backwards and the pain from the lower area of my stomach was so extreme that I could only scream. The policeman again pointed a finger at me and called me to him. I was still crying and as I walked towards him I knew that he would hit me again. I put my hands down across the lower part of my stomach so that if he hit me my stomach would receive some protection. When I got close to him he moved to the one side and kicked me hard in my stomach with the top of his foot. The blow was so hard that it went through my hands and I again fell to the floor at his feet.

Some time later the same policeman ordered all of us to back up against the wall. I was unable to stand up straight and I therefore hunched forward. The policeman came to each of us and hit our heads against the cell wall.

The same policeman then told us to take off our shoes and to

5

again stand up against the wall. He went from person to person stamping on their feet with his boots. This was terribly painful. After this had taken place the policeman left the cells.

We tried to settle down in the cell with the few materials that were available to us. After approximately 30 minutes, the same squat policeman returned as well as the one with the blazer. The one in the blazer called Victor and told him to come with them as they were going to the hospital.

The squat policeman seemed to pay very little attention to Victor and he pointed to Charles and called him to him. Charles was obviously very frightened to go to him, but he did so all the same. When he was standing in front of the squat policeman, this policeman asked for the bunch of keys from the policeman in the plain navy blue blazer and he then used these large keys to hit Charles behind the head. Charles shouted in shock and pain which had the effect of causing both the policemen to laugh and they then left the cell with Victor. The short squat policeman said he would be back that night.

I then tried to get some sleep, but could not lie on my back on the cell mat as it was still very painful and so I lay on my side with the one thin blanket that each of us had been given over me. I was very cold and kept on shivering, partly with cold and partly with pain and fear.

Since our arrest and detention that afternoon we had received no food of any kind whatsoever. I was very hungry and although we had only received water for the first time when we had been put into this cell, I felt too sick to drink very much at all. There was no toilet paper or any sort of paper which could be used when going to the one toilet that was in the adjoining cell. There was also no hot water in the cells and no soap which meant that we were unable to wash properly. My left knee was still particularly sore and the whole area of my stomach was swollen and felt very tender.

The next day, Saturday 18 October 1986, we were given breakfast early in the morning which consisted of a yellow porridge. We remained in the cell for the rest of that day. We received a mid-day and evening meal which also consisted of the same watery yellow porridge. This porridge was yellow in colour and of a texture close to water. It tasted extremely bad and most of us after eating it experienced nausea. We received no milk, tea, sugar, meat or protein of any kind during that day.

I remember that during the course of that Saturday a number of us asked certain of the policemen who had come to the cell to look at us, if we could be taken to the hospital in order to have our

6

injuries attended to. On one occasion the policeman who was asked was the same short squat policeman who had assaulted us the previous day. He refused our request.

On the following day, Sunday 19 October 1986, before we received our breakfast of yellow porridge we were all taken into another room in the police station. While we were in this room I made a statement to a policeman and told him exactly what had taken place on the day that we had been arrested. This statement was written down by the policeman who asked me to sign it. I signed it in spite of the fact that I did not see what he had written down and that he did not read it back to me.

During the course of making these statements a black policeman in blue uniform came into the room and told all of us (the six detainees) to hold out our hands. When we did this he hit us a number of times across our knuckles with a small chain and also with a small stick which appeared to be part of the handle of a broom. This was very painful and appeared to cause the police who were present in the room much amusement.

After we had given these statements to the police we received the same yellow porridge. At approximately mid-day I saw the mother of Charles along with the brother of Zachariah and the sister of Joel. They had brought clothes for certain of us. However we were not allowed to speak to them. We were consequently unable to tell them of the assaults that we had experienced since our arrest.

The food that we received on Sunday 19 October 1986 was exactly the same as we had received on Saturday, that is to say three bowls of watery yellow porridge. During the day on Sunday Victor was returned to our cell. He informed us that he had received some kind of medical treatment.

On Monday 20 October 1986 I and the six other detainees were taken to the Protea Police Station. While at this police station I made a statement to a white man, and although I did not see what he wrote and it was not read back to me, I signed it.

During the course of Monday 20 October 1986 I and certain of the other detainees were taken from the Protea Police Station to the security police building in the same area. While we were being taken to the security police building we were walking outside on the road which runs next to the police buildings. We were in single file and were led by white policemen. As we approached the security police building, I noticed my mother standing near the gate of the road leading to the security police building. She was not very close to me and although I wanted to shout to her for help, I did not do so as I feared that I would again be assaulted

7

once I was inside the building and out of her sight.

As far as I can remember I saw a doctor on Tuesday at the Protea Police Station. This doctor was white, elderly, and wore glasses. When I saw him I informed him that I had been assaulted at the Orlando Police Station on Friday and Saturday and he told me that he would write this down. I also told him that my left leg below the knee was sore and that my stomach was tender and that my back was still very sore from being hit with a hosepipe.

On Thursday 23 October 1986, I was called out of the cell and my photograph was taken by a photographer.

During the period that I was held in custody at the police cells at the Protea Police Station, I was sharing a cell with my friend Charles who is 14 years old. During this time I was not able to eat properly as each time I tried to eat I felt nauseous and on various occasions dizzy and disorientated. I found it difficult to sleep and consequently I felt very tired with the result that when the nausea occurred I often broke down crying.

I have no idea why I was arrested and detained as I have committed no illegal acts, nor been involved in any unrest or violence of any sort. I am completely bewildered and perplexed as to why I have been assaulted and mistreated by the South African police force while I have been in their custody. The treatment that I received in the Orlando Police Station, including the very poor food and other conditions in the police cells, are things which I will always remember in horror and fear.

Background to the Harare Testimony

Information drawn from Conference papers and other sources.

In September 1984 a nationwide campaign of protest and resistance to apartheid institutions was triggered. That campaign continues in various forms to this day despite a continuous State of Emergency in South Africa since 1985. It became evident soon after the start of the uprising that the police and army were directing their considerable legal and extra-legal powers at the black children in both urban and rural areas. Between 1984 and 1986:

- 312 children had been killed by the police, mostly in township confrontations
- over 1,000 children had been wounded
- an estimated 11,000 children, or 40 per cent of all detainees, had been detained under emergency laws or Emergency Regulations, provisions which deny a legal right of access to parents and lawyers

- 18,000 children had been arrested and held awaiting trial in police cells for alleged offences connected to what the South African government calls 'the unrest'

These statistics do not reveal the loss, the suffering, that the repression of children has brought. Alarmed by the nature and extent of what is now known as 'the war on children', the Bishop Ambrose Reeves Trust and the University of Zimbabwe began organising an international conference to be held in Harare in early 1987, so as to focus world attention on the plight of South Africa's youngest victims. The conference eventually took place on 24-27 September, having been postponed in response to fears of South African attacks on Zimbabwe and other Southern African countries.

The conference was remarkable for several reasons, not least being the testimony offered by a large contingent of South Africans, including child victims of brutality, their lawyers, doctors and parents.

The testimony and presentations to the conference constituted much more than a shocking catalogue of cruelty to children. The conference was also moved by the resilience of the children, their courage and defiance. While the attention of the conference remained sharply focussed on the current experience of children and on the effects of repression on them, the South African delegates reminded the conference that the source of repression was apartheid. It appeared from their testimony that the children do not regard themselves as 'innocent victims', but that they plead 'guilty' to engaging in the protest campaigns in townships and schools to change apartheid. To call for detained children to be 'charged or released' is therefore not enough. It may mean only that children are charged under a harsh legal system and sentenced to serve terms of imprisonment for acts of legitimate resistance. It may mean that children would be released only to find themselves in a larger prison, apartheid South Africa, which promises them poverty, discrimination and inferior educational facilities. It may mean that children would be released but their parents would continue to be detained. It may mean that children in South Africa would be released but that the hundreds of thousands of children in neighbouring Angola and Mozambique would continue to suffer violence and starvation as a result of apartheid's policies.

In linking the repression of children in South Africa to the policies of apartheid, the South African delegates asked the conference to consider the kind of society that could so directly brutalise its young, and also the conditions in that society which

9

compelled its children to assume the adult risks of protest and resistance, to forgo their childhood. It is appropriate to give a thumb-nail sketch of the conditions under which children live in South Africa

Apartheid – A Larger Prison

In background papers placed before the conference, facts and figures indicated that black children in South Africa have to contend with structural deprivation throughout their lives: poverty and discrimination in a land of affluence and plenty. Set out below is just a part of the information contained in the conference papers and in other sources, all of them listed in the section on sources at the end of the book.

- For African children in South Africa the struggle to survive begins at birth. The infant mortality rate for African infants is 80 out of every 1,000. For whites it is 13. Coloured and African children are 14 times more likely to die before the age of 5 than white children. Black children are affected by diseases that are a direct result of poverty (kwashiorkor, tuberculosis, gastro-enteritis) or diseases which with limited efforts could be eradicated (measles). One-third of African, Coloured and Asian children below the age of 14 are underweight and stunted. Diet for people in many rural areas is worse than it was for their grandparents. While on the one hand South Africa exports food, on the other hand school children in one district – Clanwilliam – were reported to be regularly fainting from hunger. According to a 1980 survey, in cases where an African child survives the first five years, his or her life expectancy is 9 years less than that of a white child.
- Children in the rural areas suffer more markedly than their urban contemporaries. They often have no male parent present as the men are compelled to take up migrant labour in the mines or urban industries. Eighty-six per cent of children with kwashiorkor surveyed in the Transkei bantustan in 1984 had an absent migrant father, and 62 per cent had both parents absent.
- Many rural children are compelled to help maintain the family by seeking work at an early age. There is no law against child labour. Most of such children work on white farms where the hours are long and the pay derisory – as low as £1 a month or nothing at all. But even in urban areas poverty forces most children to abandon schooling at an early age.
- The poverty that affects the health of rural black South Africans is also apparent in the urban setting. High unemployment,

10

discriminatory health and welfare services, a low wage structure for semi-skilled and unskilled workers, the absence of basic social amenities such as recreational facilities, electricity or tarred roads, all contribute to the poverty of townships. Undoubtedly one of the major exacerbating factors in reducing the quality of urban life is the housing shortage. This is all the more noteworthy because it is the result of a conscious policy since the 1960s to limit the number of black people living outside the rural areas. Currently there is a shortage of 679,000 houses for black people in the urban areas, yet there is a surplus of 37,000 houses in the segregated white group areas. The effect on the privacy of the residents of three or four families sharing one four or perhaps six-roomed house is obvious. One township of 1,800 houses has no telephone, post office, park, sportsfield or bank. These townships stand in stark contrast to the nearby white suburbs which rank among the most affluent in the world.

- Many parents are forced to take up residence in dormitory areas far away from their places of employment and to commute daily. In the case of Kwandebele, for example, this involves up to 8 hours of bussing every working day. Such parents will hardly see their children despite living under the same roof.
- The law is viewed by South Africa's black population as being largely an oppressive mechanism, almost wholly ineffective in dealing with township crime and mostly concerned to crush political dissent. It is seen as discriminatory in intention and application, and this view is shared by black children as pointed out in a conference paper by Pius Langa. On the other hand the law is unmitigatingly harsh on those black people it seeks to prosecute. More specifically it fails to protect children who are in the dock adequately, according to Prof McQuoid Mason in another conference paper.
- Black children who wish to alter the odds against them by effecting political changes constitutionally find that the South African constitution denies them any political vote in parliament, either now or in the future. Extra-parliamentary pressure, including peaceful demonstrations, has been effectively outlawed.

Against this background of poverty and political frustration, black South Africans have placed a premium on educational advancement, and have channelled much energy into improving the quality of black education. In 1953 the black community greeted with dismay the announcement by Prime Minister HF Verwoerd that he would introduce a separate educational system for African children because 'there is no place for him [the bantu] in the European community above certain forms of labour'. The system of 'bantu' education has meant that:

- Education is expensive for blacks, yet compulsory and virtually free for whites; the per capita expenditure in 1985-6 was R365 for Africans, R2,374 for whites:
- The student teacher ratio in 1982 was 18:1 for whites, and 41:1 for Africans (and in some areas as high as 150:1)
- In 1986, 40-50 per cent of the African population was functionally illiterate
- 69 per cent of African teachers have not themselves completed schooling
- In 1978 only 4 of every 100 children who had started school actually stayed in school till the final year of education. The figure for whites was 69. More than half of the children who drop out do so with less than four years of primary school education.
- Classrooms are overcrowded, schools far from home, facilities scarce, the education is authoritarian and teachers rely on corporal punishment to maintain discipline.
- When children leave school they find that the promise of advancement is largely an empty one. Unemployment in 1981 was conservatively estimated at 21 per cent. It is considerably worse now, and the brunt is borne by women and school leavers. Education plays little part in getting what employment is available, which is generally unskilled and low paid. For those who do not get employment the prospects are bleak. In the Eastern Cape many school leavers will never obtain employment at all.
- As Eric Molobi points out in his presentation in Part 3, education has been a focal point of black resistance, particularly amongst the children themselves. In June 1976 students protested against being made to study certain subjects in Afrikaans. In the ensuing confrontation with the police an estimated 1,000 students were killed, mostly as a result of the police use of firearms. From 1980 to 1986 students protested against the inferior quality of the education, the authoritarian nature of school instruction and the racist content of the curricula. The Congress of South African Students (COSAS), the organisation responsible for articulating these grievances, was outlawed in 1985.

Children and Repression

When the widespread protests against apartheid erupted in 1984, the government and its repressive forces apparently believed that the backbone of the resistance could be broken by a sustained maximum-force policy directed mainly at children and young adolescents. The range of repressive strategies employed by government agencies between 1984 and 1986 is described in Haysom's presentation. They range from harsh township policing, mass detentions and licensing vigilante squads, to the more sophisticated reconstruction of township politics. Available information indicates that children bore a great part of the effect of the repressive policies, as they had done since 1976 and before.

Between 1984 and the present, children have been in the frontline of a mass sustained and national challenge to apartheid institutions and have had to pay a terrible price for it.

Children throughout the country have died as a result of the police use of lethal firearms including combat rifles. The total number of children killed by police up to the end of 1986 was well over 312. This figures excludes the considerable number who have died in 1987, who have been killed by bantustan forces, by vigilantes, the South African Defence Force (SADF) or the Municipal Police. Monitoring groups report that many of those killed, are killed by reckless and indiscriminate firing and others in situations such as attending illegal gatherings or stonethrowing. When police fired at a funeral procession at Langa in the Eastern Cape on 21 March 1985, 19 out of 20 persons killed were shot in the back or side. Nearly 50 per cent of the victims were juveniles. During 1985 the Empilisweni clinic at Crossroads squatter camp treated 500 persons shot by the police. Over 10 per cent were under the age of 15 – the youngest was only 5 years old. A medical journal report stated that 55 of 93 persons shot dead had been shot in the back; of these 11 were under 15 years of age. A study of 77 children killed by the police in 1985 revealed that 19 victims were under 11 years of age. As noted above over 1,000 children were wounded between 1984 and 1986, according to police statistics which reflect only a part of the whole picture.

It is estimated that 10,000 children, 40 per cent of all detainees, have been detained without trial under provisions which deny a legal right of access to parents or lawyers, and do not discriminate between the conditions of detention for adults and children. Children have been held in large communal cells, their education has been disrupted and they have been denied full recreational amenities. At one stage it was reported that male convicted

13

common-law prisoners were sexually abusing child detainees, though it appears that since then most detainees have been segregated from convicts. Parents are not automatically informed of the detention of their children and have to go to considerable lengths to ascertain if their children are being detained, and if so, where they are being held.

- A total of 18,000 children were arrested between 1984 and 1986 on charges relating to protests and 'unrest'. Approximately 20 per cent of these have been convicted and in general the sentences have been severe. In some cases children have been sentenced to lengthy terms of imprisonment (several years) for minor offences, which in most countries would have received only a nominal punishment. As lawyer Johnny de Lange points out in Part 2, the sentences handed down in many rural areas are shocking, particularly given the youthfulness of the accused. These children are often not legally represented. Furthermore, even those eventually acquitted may have spent many months in custody because, as in the case of 11-year-old Fanie Guduka, a magistrate holds that they are 'a threat to society'. Guduka spent 59 days in custody.
- Children have been subjected to violence both at the time of arrest and later in custody. The affidavits and testimonies gathered by the DPSC, the New York-based Lawyers Committee for Human Rights, and the University of Cape Town Institute of Criminology indicate systematic assaults and the frequent use of chilling torture techniques such as strangulation and electric shocks. These allegations were not only corroborated by individual victims such as those who testified at the conference but also by Doctors Orr and Foster, who presented papers based on the evidence collected by them for a court case brought by Orr and a book by Foster. It is only necessary here to say that Dr Orr's evidence suggested that 40 per cent of those detained during the initial stage of the 1985 State of Emergency in the Eastern Cape were assaulted. It should also be noted that since 1963, over 60 persons have died while in detention, and since 1984, 26 persons have died while in police custody. Of these, 9 were between 13 and 20 years of age.
- The long-term psychological effects on children exposed to violence are hard to estimate and varies from child to child. For some, the stress of living under the curfew regulations, the insecurity arising out of the army and police patrols, the visual exposure to scenes of violent confrontation, can cause extreme anxiety and associated neuroses. For others the mental scars from detention or assaults or both, manifest themselves in

classic post-traumatic stress disorders (anxiety, nightmares, panic, bedwetting) or in the erosion of feelings of empathy and care.

- For many children the most traumatic experience is not their own detention, but the detention of parents and older siblings. The South African delegates were concerned that protest against the repression of children should not in any way legitimise or lessen international condemnation of the repressive violence directed at adults.

- It is also important to recognise the effects on families, and the broader community, of the repression of children. The example of the mass detention of children profoundly disturbs older family members and may even pit an anxious parent against a more defiant child. The repression of children can be used to control an entire community.

- Finally, mention must be made of the hardship which refugee children endure. Many children abandon their families and their society to escape from South Africa. The conference was given an insights into some of their problems by doctors who work with exiled children. For countless others their exile is internal, hiding out in villages and cities far from their homes for months or even years.

The Frontline States

Angola and Mozambique are wracked by war in which locally-based forces are receiving direct support from the South African Defence Force and the United States in the case of Angola and in the case of Mozambique are trained, equipped and recruited by South Africans. Regional destabilisation became the key foreign policy strategy of the South African regime precisely because it weakens South Africa's neighbours and paralyses their capacity to forge independent economies and effective government. Destabilisation is a regional policy and extends beyond these two strife-torn countries whose economies have been systematically sabotaged. Zimbabwe, Lesotho, Botswana, Zambia and Swaziland have all had to contend with both economic pressures and SADF strikes into their capital cities. Many of the raids, supposedly directed at the ANC's military wing, have taken the lives of innocent nationals, non-combatants and refugees. The raids have the character of reprisal attacks, symbolic exercises to threaten neighbouring governments and their subjects. The destabilisation of the region has had a colossal effect on the lives of children in the region.

- Children have suffered directly as a result of cross-border raids by South African forces. In the Kassinga attack, for instance, the SADF killed the inhabitants of a refugee camp in Angola. After the soldiers had finished, 167 unarmed women and 298 children lay dead. A more recent example was provided by Nthabiseng Mabusa, a 13-year-old girl who gave testimony at the Harare Conference. She was at her aunt's home in Gaberone, Botswana, at 8 pm on 14 June 1986. A masked soldier burst into the home, shooting the occupants with an automatic firearm. Nthabiseng ran outside and was shot in the stomach and in the back by another soldier. She is now paralysed from the waist down for life.
- Children have suffered, particularly in Angola and Mozambique, as a direct result of the wars carried on by the South African-backed forces. A Unicef report published in 1987 estimates that Mozambique alone has suffered an average of 10,000 deaths a year as a direct result of the war since 1981.
- The most devastasting cause of death and disability to children is the indirect effect of the war. To take the Mozambique case, 42 per cent of its precarious budget allocations goes to defence; 40 per cent of schools and 25 per cent of classes have been destroyed by the MNR forces. Transport routes, energy and food supply lines have been cut off. Primary health care gains have been reversed and programmes abandoned. Half the rural population has been displaced or forced to flee as a result of the destruction of villages, crops, farmhouses, shops and roads. Poverty, and the channelling of available resources in defence, have prevented water and sanitation programmes and drought relief aid from getting to rural areas. The country is unable to raise its export earnings. Food production is falling. The consequences are dire for children. In the drought of 1983-4 an estimated 100,000 persons died. In addition the under-5 infant mortality rate, which from the initial post-independence trend should be comparable to Tanzania's at about 180, has reached 375 per 1,000 live births. Taking all these factors into account, including the excess child mortality rates, the Unicef report estimates that between 1980 and 1986 the destabilisation of Angola and Mozambique has cost the lives of half a million infants and children. The total cost to the children in terms of malnutrition, stunted growth, fear and daily poverty is unquantifiable. It was in this context that Reverend Frank Chikane, in his speech to the conference, stressed that the problems of South African children cannot be treated separately from the children suffering in the Front Line States.

The Harare Conference

It was against this background that the conference in Zimbabwe took place. The very fact that it took place at all can be regarded as a gesture of defiance. Harare is a short flight from Pretoria, and is vulnerable to economic and military reprisals. The conference had been postponed once after South Africa had made one of its regular threats against the Frontline States, threats which have often been followed by attacks and raids. The challenge to Pretoria in holding such a conference in Southern Africa was sharpened by the presence of two South African groups: the one, a senior and impressive delegation from the African National Congress's headquarters including ANC president Oliver Tambo; the other from inside the country, numbering nearly 150, more than half the total number of South Africans at the conference. For both groups there were risks in attending. ANC personnel have been assassinated in Harare and there have been attacks and bombings of ANC offices in the city. Those who came from South Africa ran the risk of unknown reactions from the South African government upon their return – detention, interrogation, confiscation of passports. Beyers Naude asked the conference to consider especially those who were not as well known as himself, those who were not protected by professional status or international reputation. In fact at least seven delegates were questioned upon their return. More recently a boy whose account of his six months in detention was featured in a television documentary shown in the United States was identified by police, questioned and released. On 26 January 1988, five days after his interrogation, his body was found in a field. He had been shot in the head.

Much of the testimony given at the conference is presented here – some of it is drawn from background documents submitted to the conference, and some of it from edited transcripts of statements. There are also sections containing responses to the conference of people who participated in it.

Harare Days and Nights
– Impressions of the Conference

Victoria Brittain

South Africa's townships greeted Oliver Tambo, President of the African National Congress, with, first a stunned silence at the sight of the man, and then an outpouring of emotion in tears,

17

laughter, hugs, song and dance to the legend who has sustained a generation.

Mothers, priests, lawyers, doctors, community organisers who had travelled from all over South Africa to Harare in September 1987 had come there to expose to the world the nightmare of repression and torture that engulfs their children. Oliver Tambo, and half the National Executive Committee of the ANC, were perhaps the last people many of them had expected to find there to listen to the grim stories of the apartheid regime which, to survive, has targeted black youth as one of the mainstays of resistance.

From the spontaneous first moments of welcome as Oliver Tambo was whirled off his feet by the crowd from inside the country, the myths about individuals in the long-exiled ANC leadership began to drop away and were replaced by an open dialogue between the stifled internal and external power centres of South Africa which only days before would have been unimaginable.

It was a dialogue on many levels between people who often knew almost nothing about each other at first hand, but nonetheless reacted as though to bonds of comradeship forged in the frontline of what has become a state of war. Behind this striking phenomenon of trust lies the invisible presence of the outlawed ANC in the townships these delegates came from − where its banned literature is sought out, and its policies known and discussed, its flag and colours sported as a defiant morale-booster at funerals of victims of police violence which are mass political rallies, its leaders' names, Mandela, Tambo, Slovo, woven into the resistance songs of everyday life. But all this had not prepared people for the emotional shock of the freedom of face-to-face meetings.

The skills and knowledge of the internal and external groups are, each knows, complementary. For the first time, for many, in Harare each could measure themselves directly in the eyes of the other. The distorted pictures created by the South African regime's expensive propaganda machine had not only worked internationally, but also had had its effect both on each side's subconscious idea of the other and on the self-images of both. The impact of meeting stripped all that away.

The holding of the Harare Conference was in itself an indictment of the local and, especially, of the international media's failure in reporting the situation in South Africa. The attention of the world beyond South Africa had not been focussed on the government's systematic attack on black children as the present (and to the regime, even more frighteningly, the uncontrollable future) challengers of the apartheid state. This major strand of contemporary history lay half-buried. The censorship imposed by Pretoria under the successive States of Emergency had succeeded. Throughout the world, newspapers, radio and television had grown used to blunting reality to conform to the rules of a state long outlawed from most of the international community.

Laying bare the numbed indifference of those who should have told his story long since, and the immense courage of the mother who brought him to Harare, an 11-year-old boy wriggled away from the microphone muttering, 'I don't want to say more, Vlok will get me'. The Minister of Law and Order, Adriaan Vlok, loomed unbearably large in the first day of such children's testimony, which had even someone like the church leader Frank Chikane, who confronts such evidence daily, leaving the hall in tears.

That wary, restless, 11-year-old epitomised Pretoria's attempted destruction of his life-hopes and the very fabric of his society. Pretoria has indelibly marked that child's present and future. He and so many others unveiled at Harare the undreamed-of human resources which, as in every other revolutionary situation in history, these extraordinary South African times had brought out.

The terror of armed police and soldiers, or local vigilante groups acting for the state, breaking into family homes in the middle of the night, of the children taken away to unknown destinations, of the physical and psychological violence which have become a new norm for black children and their families, were burned into the minds of everyone at Harare. The mother of that child had three other children, including a teenage girl, in detention. The quiet desperation of her description of begging at one police station after another to be allowed to see them, and the slanting focus of her anxiety on the one fact that they had not written their exams, was so painful to see that it was hard to meet her eyes.

Sitting attentively to one side throughout the hours of personal testimony of victims and the scarcely less anguished analysis by doctors, lawyers, priests and community organisers, was the ANC's Oliver Tambo. Like their acknowledged leader, head of a popular government in exile, he was the first focus of each speaker. 'Mr President,' they began. Little of the detail of the pain inflicted on individual children or the brutal crushing of whole communities could have been new to Tambo, but as the days wore on he grew perceptibly graver. As one of the other ANC leaders put it, 'these days it is not easy being a South African leader; the burden of people's expectations gets heavier with every new phase of repression.'

The ANC was represented by many of the historic generation who, like President Tambo, Treasurer Thomas Nkobi, Ruth Mompati, Gertrude Shope and Joe Slovo, Secretary-General of the South African Communist Party, had carried the burden of two decades of leadership from exile. These were the people who, in the early 1960s when all seemed lost and the organisation smashed, had inspired the Algerian President Ahmed Ben Bella's famous speech to all Africa, 'let us die a little' for the liberation of South Africa. In 1963 an ANC office was opened in Algiers and men like Johnstone Makatini began to travel the world on Algerian passports spreading the knowledge which would begin ousting the South African regime from the international community.

The stars of the new generation of ANC leaders were there too, products of a different period and different experiences, many of which were interwoven with those of former comrades re-met in Harare from township organisations. Steve Tshwete, for instance, a senior ANC official, spent 15 years on Robben Island for sabotage and furthering the aims of the ANC and used the time it to give himself the education the likes of which an impoverished black child like him could never have dreamed. Tshwete speaks of Camus, Zola, Shakespeare, Tolstoy and Picasso as the intimate friends who peopled his days on the Island, and then strengthened him as an organiser of the United Democratic Front (UDF) two steps ahead of the police until his narrow escape from the country in October 1985.

Younger than him there was another generation meeting again with old friends from old battles started when they were all no more than children. Thousands of young men and women fled South Africa in 1976 in the wake of the Soweto massacre of schoolchildren. Many of their families and friends never even knew whether they were dead or alive after that traumatic period which so fractured their lives. Some of them were in the ANC's delegation of 60 people in Harare now with responsible jobs in the external mission.

The conference illustrated in these young men the triumph of the ANC's long and often bitter battle for their long-time vision and strategy of non-racialism. At Harare it was reaffirmed from many political perspectives as a central principle in the South African struggle. The Muslim Imam Faried Esack of The Call of Islam, a UDF affiliate, for instance, in a tribute to the ANC

20

leadership and Archbishop Trevor Huddleston, convenor of the conference, said 'thank you for preventing our struggle from degenerating into a black versus white confrontation, thank you for standing with us for truth versus falsehood, thank you for standing with us for justice versus injustice.'

Among the young ANC generation, as among young delegates from inside the country, were plenty of people who were fired by the black consciousness movement as a rallying point in the darkest days of resistance. Many forces had attempted in the post-1976 upheavals to co-opt its energies and set part of the forces of resistance against the ANC because of its anti-imperialist commitment and its alliance with the South African Communist Party. At Harare so many exchanges of personal histories by people who had been separated by the upheavals of the struggle for years underlined to everyone the extensive attempts at promoting division and how they had misfired. Intellectual struggles of the young self-educated township leaders detained with the ANC leadership, including Nelson Mandela himself on Robben Island, had changed their politics. And for the young exiles, too, the impact of the first face-to-face meetings with the ANC transformed their ideas about the nature of politics. Steve Tshwete expressed clearly their new perspective: 'The politics of colour are a very devastating instrument in the hands of imperialist countries, and all reactionaries.'

After the conference's formal sessions in the Harare International Conference Centre, at every meal, every meeting at the bar, every night-time gathering, all these different strands of opposition to Pretoria met in an unfolding political event, part spontaneous, part structured. The success of the white regime's censorship, banning of books, banning of people, banning of meetings over so many years, meant that many of the delegates from inside the country were coming to Harare with only the limited experience of a fragment of their own closed society. Many of them came from provinces and towns separated not only by hundreds of miles, but also by the central factor of their lives – apartheid.

The Freedom Charter might be the theoretical foundation of most of their political beliefs since the UDF began its long discussions about formally adopting it, but in the daily consuming struggle for survival there were many who had never had the space or time to imagine life shaped upon it. And there were many individuals there not as part of any organisation, but driven by personal experiences which had triggered a deep rejection of the system. The Harare days became a precious foretaste of a post-apartheid society. Colour, status, power-structure rules were deliberately and joyfully forgotten – for those four days.

The new freedom was electric and its fleeting nature made it all the more poignant. For many it was the first taste of liberation from the abnormal society of South Africa in which they had all learned to survive by making completely abnormal demands on their creativity and courage. No one wanted to sleep, or to lose a moment of the tidal wave of questions, ideas, impressions, mutual exchanges, which stunned every one of the 600 or so delegates.

That a such delicate interplay of mutual respect and mutual trust could mark a meeting of people whose lives had been so deliberately imbued with precisely the opposite experiences is something no outsider can explain.

The strength of the organisation of the ANC, rebuilt since the traumatic toll on the internal network of the Rivonia trial 20 years before, was shown at Harare with an openness the banned organisation has never chosen to display before. But in Harare the ANC was responding, face to face for the first time, to a diverse group of South African exiles and to a cross-section of individuals from many political backgrounds inside the country. The coherence and consistency of the latter was all the more impressive because they were mostly people not from the top leadership but from the secondary leadership level. Many of the best-known names of leaders of legal organisations, such as the UDF, were in prison or underground. And the older internal leaders, towering figures from the Congress in the 1950s who had survived the prison terms, the torture, the bannings, the bereavements, and the escalating state violence of more than two decades, were mostly unable to be there.

Behind the atmosphere of these meetings lay unspoken respect for the different intensities of others' experiences. Years in exile have killed plenty of liberation movements, from internecine plotting, if not from the creeping paralysis of individual despair. Long years of bleak hotel rooms, cramped offices, underfunded diplomatic campaigns seemingly making little impact in an indifferent international context where only power now counts, poor communications, and manifold disappointments, make exiles easy targets for spies and traitors. The ANC has suffered from its share of all this, but has withstood the corrosive effects. UDF leaders have had to cope with a transition to operating in conditions of clandestinity, which have often enough in history been so stressful and shortlived that individuals bring their own exposure either by paranoia or by an over-optimistic carelessness.

On the opening day of the conference, before the welcome

speech by Prime Minister Robert Mugabe, long neat lines of Zimbabwean schoolchildren filled the upper galleries of the hall. Their trim uniforms, sturdy bodies and carefree childish whispering bespoke another world from the one of terror and repression their South African contemporaries would unveil to them. Although these Zimbabwean children were mostly too young to know what it had meant to fight a war for their independence from a racist regime, their respectful response to these other children from an even more terrifying war waged on them by the government was a moving display of how deep within the societies of the Front Line States solidarity springs.

The strength and dignity of the South African children showed everyone the calibre of future South African leaders. Their open dedication to their fellow South Africans is the clearest possible demonstration of the utter failure of the apartheid regime's policies of withholding deliberately from them education and a quality of social life which twentieth-century civilisation would call normal. Their demand for 'Freedom or Death' is literal – the expression of the patriotic self-sacrifice these young people have prepared themselves for.

'The child is not dead'

From the statement which Oliver Tambo, President of the African National Congress, made at the opening of the conference

The Afrikaner poet, Ingrid Jonker, died in 1965 at the young age of 32. Consumed by a dark foreboding and overwhelmed by despair, she committed suicide as her creative intellect was coming to its ripening. By her death, she joined herself to the children of our country about whom she had written. Her tragic passing was as powerful an indictment of the apartheid system as were these verses which she has left us, and I quote:

> The child is not dead
> the child lifts his fists against his mother
> who shouts Afrika! shouts the breath
> of freedom and the veld
> in the locations of the cordoned heart. . .

> The child is not dead
> not at Langa nor at Nyanga
> nor at Orlando nor at Sharpeville
> nor at the police post at Philippi
> where he lies with a bullet through his brain

23

The child is the dark shadow of the soldiers
on guard with their rifles, saracens and batons
the child is present at all assemblies and law-giving
the child peers through the windows of houses and into
  the hearts of mothers
this child who wanted only to play in the sun at
  Nyanga is everywhere
the child is grown to a man and treks on through all
  Africa
the child grown into a giant journeys over the whole
  world

Without a pass

We share with Ingrid Jonker that noble vision of the child who wanted only to play in the sun, the child grown into a giant, journeying over the whole world, without a pass. We share with her the knowledge and confidence that the wanton massacre of the children at Langa and at Nyanga, at Orlando and at Sharpeville, at Soweto, Athlone, Maseru, Gaborone, Harare, Maputo, the knowledge that this succession of massacres will not deny us our journey over the whole world – free at last, at last free, perhaps the last to be free but free, at last.

What pain it must have been to her, who, being an Afrikaner, saw these images, the images of those who immolated the child who wanted only to play in the sun at Nyanga, and then told her that they murdered in order to protect her, her kind and her so-called 'civilisation'. And what her torment to know that each extra day of her so-called 'way of life' cost the souls of many a black child.

And under that terrible order the children die, with bullets through their heads, welts on their bodies, hearts and brains stopped before they could attain maturity, because a person as ordinary as you and I, has inherited powers that go beyond all that is permissible in the conduct of relations among those we would all count as mortal.

A criminal tyranny that has the audacity to call itself a civilisation lives on across the borders of this country, Zimbabwe. It survives because humanity, and principally ourselves, has not yet said that an extra day of apartheid is an extra day too long. It thrives because it can include within its body count the lives of children whom it describes as opponents that it has vanquished. It persists because without the death of the innocents, it cannot be.

We meet here today because we want to discuss the unspeakable plight of the black children of South Africa. We meet, the children of South Africa and the children of Zimbabwe sitting together in this hall, people from South Africa and people from around the world sitting together in this hall, we meet because there is something that is happening to the hapless and the innocent that should not be allowed to happen. We meet because we recognise that our own lives have meaning only to the extent that they are used to create a social condition which will make the lives of the children happy, full and meaningful. We have gathered ourselves in Harare and on this particular occasion because we know that a grievous injustice is being done to all humanity.

And yet, strange as it might seem, there are some who are opposed to the fact that we meet here, for these purposes. These are convinced that our consultation is of the devil's own making. And yet they are the first to stand unabashed in front of the whole world, projecting themselves as the very representation of all that is good, upright and unconquerable.

Our century has witnessed some of the worst atrocities in all human history, perpetrated by people who considered themselves good, upright and unconquerable. But in the end humanity has itself judged these, regardless of their opinion of themselves. And once more the peoples have judged that those who uphold the apartheid system are committing a crime against humanity itself. And as this conference knows, at the core of this crime is the theory and practice of racism.

What more man-hating ideology can there be than this which defines black people as less than human! And could we expect any consequences from its practice other than the slaughter of black children? The predator feeds on human blood. That fact defines its being.

The endless rows of children's graves, ready, prepared, for the children whose death by disease and starvation is planned according to defined statistical regularities, marks the true essence of this system. The barefoot child – clothed in a sack that should carry produce – planting, hoeing, reaping, is the alter ego of the white farmer who towers above the toddler with a whip in his hand. The orphan is no more than a precise statement that apartheid lives. The mangled remains of the black child who wanted only to play in the sun are the justification for the existence of the largest and most sophisticated machinery of repression that Africa has ever known. The apartheid predator feeds on human blood. That fact defines its being.

This terrible desolation defines for us what our struggle must be

25

about. We cannot be true liberators unless the liberation we will achieve guarantees all children the rights to life, health, happiness and free development, respecting the individuality, the inclinations and capabilities of each child. Our liberation would be untrue to itself if it did not, among its first tasks, attend to the welfare of the millions of children whose lives have been stunted and turned into a terrible misery by the violence of the apartheid system.

Moreover, our concern for the children, the inheritors of our future, cannot be postponed until the day we achieve our emancipation.

The Political Context of the War against Children

Frank Chikane, Secretary-General of the South African Council of Churches and a vice-president of the United Democratic Front (UDF) – he has been detained three times and in 1985 he was acquitted on all charges of high treason of which he and 15 other UDF leaders had been accused.

I bring greetings on behalf of all South Africans (except the white-minority regime) to Comrade President Mugabe, the people of Zimbabwe, and all the leaders and people of the Front Line States. We know how much your stand against this barbaric inhuman system has cost you in terms of human life, economic and political destabilisation. We know the way in which the forces of reaction are using hunger as a political weapon at the expense of hundreds of thousands of our brothers and sisters in the whole Southern African region.

The oppressed masses of South Africa take your pain, suffering and death for their sakes seriously. Your injury is their injury. Your pain, their pain, and whenever you are attacked they feel more obliged to fight vehemently against the system to speed up its demise.

The apartheid regime has turned this region of Southern Africa into a region of refugees and exiles. It has plunged it into a war which is fought on various fronts: from Luanda to Maputo, from Lusaka to Cape Town. We cannot allow this situation to continue without an end. We need to turn this sub-continent into a united homeland where all will live in peace and prosperity. We need to free the economic potential of this region, not just to benefit the people of Southern Africa, but the whole African continent, even the world.

The war against children in South Africa is taking place within this context of conflict and destabilisation. We have come here to share our pain and suffering, particularly of our children. We just hope that there are still people in the world who have enough moral instinct to be moved by our witness to act decisively and make it impossible for the apartheid regime to live a day longer. We also hope that those who collude with this inhuman regime will be ashamed of their action and withdraw their support for the system.

The children of South Africa, particularly black children, are denied their right to be children. Children in our country are violently forced by the conditions in the country to be adults before their time. They are put in a situation where they have to make *decisions* which are normally made by adults. They are forced to make *choices* which they should not make at their age. They are made to fight *battles* they should not be fighting as children.

They also want to have a chance to be children and develop naturally like other children. They want to play hide and seek. They want to role-play mothers and fathers and play games like other children.

Their normal and natural growth as children has been and is being violently disrupted, forcing them to be adults before their time.

I want to concentrate on the context of war against the voteless majority in South Africa. To understand the form this war is taking today and the nature of the crisis we are facing we need to trace its origin over the last decade of struggle in our country.

There was a change in state strategy in the late seventies. This shift did not help the apartheid regime. Instead it deepened the crisis and the contradictions within the system. The States of Emergency which commenced in 1985 and in which our children have been so badly brutalised, are the culmination of that crisis.

The independence of Mozambique and Angola in 1975 altered the balance of forces in the Southern African region. It broke the so-called 'cordon sanitaire' of white-ruled colonies which gave the regime a feeling of security and confidence. The fall of the Portuguese colonies brought the battle-front against colonial and neo-colonial rule closer to the heartland of white oppression and exploitation.

This created a succession of problems for South Africa: the 1976

27

The international character of participants at this conference is a very clear manifestation of the universality of the feeling of revulsion and concern generated by the dehumanisation to which the majority of the people of South Africa are daily subjected by the apartheid system in that country. I sincerely hope that the deliberations of this conference will enhance international awareness of the terrible plight and situation of the weakest and most vulnerable of the South African population, namely, the children, the black children who are, as we know, the most hapless and helpless victims of the evil monster that is apartheid. It is they who are daily malnourished by apartheid, they who are daily miseducated by apartheid, and they who above all, are daily jailed, maimed and murdered by apartheid.

Yet, international awareness of the suffering of the children in apartheid South Africa is alone not adequate unless it is followed by a resolve, determination and strength to fight and eradicate the heinous system from our civilised world. The pariah state of South Africa has no legitimate claim to being part of the civilised international community as long as the sanctity and respect for the rule of law has not been restored in that country.

The prisons of South Africa are today full of children who, under civilised conditions should be in schools undergoing preparation for their future roles and responsibilities as citizens of their country. Alas, their prescribed lot is that of being murdered, tortured, brutalised and imprisoned.

Most of us from this region know that the rule of law does not exist in apartheid South Africa. The law, such as exists there, is only for the advancement and protection of the privileges of the few. The law and all the related state institutions have been designed and geared to protect and promote the interests of the white minority by systematically trampling upon even the most basic rights of the black masses.

Should any voice of conscience draw attention to the injustice of the system and criticise the so-called law enforcement agents, such criticism is contemptuously ignored. Recently, the Detainees' Parents Support Committee published its informative reports or studies on tortures and detentions in the 1980s. The reaction of the racist Minister of Law and Order was characteristic. He accused the Committee of vilifying the police. Mr Vlok and all the members of his apartheid regime are evidently men to whom conscience and morality are mere trifles.

The Honourable Prime Minister of Zimbabwe, Robert G Mugabe, at the opening session

Soweto uprising followed by the November 1977 UN Security Council resolution on mandatory arms embargo against South Africa; the guerrilla actions of the ANC which were fuelled by the Soweto uprising; the economic decline from 1974 up to 1978; the substantial outflow of foreign capital. All these factors deepened the crisis. White hegemony was clearly under siege.

In response to this crisis the regime produced the 1977 Defence White Paper which laid the basis for PW Botha's concept of a total onslaught from beyond South Africa's borders. This 'total onslaught' needed a 'total national strategy'. The 'total onslaught' which South Africa was said to be facing was presented as a communist conspiracy.

This formulation has two advantages for white South Africa. Firstly, it allows all criticism of apartheid to be dismissed as communist. Secondly, it creates a condition which makes both white South Africans and the West see South Africa as the last bastion against communism, the protector of Western Christian values. It created a serious contradiction for the West, so that any attacks on apartheid by them would be said to be of assistance to the Soviet Union.

The 'total strategy' to counter this 'total onslaught' had three main elements.

Firstly, there was a need to forge some kind of national unity government to defend white rule. The present tri-cameral system developed from the need of the racist regime to draft sections of the so-called Indian and Coloured populations in South Africa and some middle-class Africans into a junior partnership with the white minority against the black majority. It was an attempt to pit one group of people against the other.

Secondly, 'total strategy' involved vigorous repression of all opponents of the system.

Thirdly, South Africa sought hegemony over the whole Southern African region to silence those opposed to apartheid and to neutralise the African National Congress guerrilla warfare against South Africa. This would consist of a combination of diplomatic, political, economic and military strategies.

The total strategy, therefore, was aimed at establishing South Africa's position as a 'regional power' and establishing a 'constellation of states' under its tutelage. This would require a 'common approach' on both the security and economic fronts against what was called expanding communist influence of the region.

The third leg of this total strategy was frustrated by the independence of Zimbabwe and by the formation of the Southern

African Development Co-ordination Conference (SADCC) dashing the hope of forming the Constellation of Southern African States.

To understand the context of the war in South Africa we need therefore to look at the first two legs of the *total strategy*, that is, *reform* and *repression*. It is now a matter of history that the oppressed masses of South Africa saw through the fraud of these reforms. They organised against them and defeated them.

At best, the reform strategies helped the people to mobilise and organise against the subtle attempt to further entrench apartheid and maintain white domination. This campaign, led mainly by the UDF, galvanised the masses and transformed the face of politics in South Africa.

The political complexion of this country was rapidly altered as mass organisation spread like a veldfire. Throughout the country, from the smallest village to the largest cities, the people organised themselves into democratic structures which expressed their needs and aspirations. These structures (street committees, education committees, people's courts, etc.) were declared subversive by the regime because they stood opposed to government apartheid structures.

The arrogance of the system in ignoring the popular rejection of the tri-cameral system and in imposing the new structures of oppression (after the so-called Coloured and Indian elections of August 1984) created an explosive situation which ignited in the Vaal in September 1984. This event sparked off a wave of uprisings around the country, leaving the government-created local authorities in shambles. The police and those perceived as collaborators and informers were forced out of the townships except when they came in on military or security operations.

In short the people simply refused to collaborate or co-operate in their own oppression. They refused to be governed by the apartheid regime.

The state then resorted to the second leg of the total strategy, that is *repression*. The army and the police occupied the townships. Thousands of our people were killed, many thousands were detained, many of them tortured. And all this was directed mainly against young people under the age of 25. Many of these were children under the age of 18. But the vicious attacks on the people by the state only served to increase the militancy and anger of the people, particularly young people. The government then declared a State of Emergency between July 1985 and March 1986 which was reimposed in June 1986 and continues today. The South African Defence Force, a machine of war, was sent into the townships, the schools, the villages, in every part of the country.

Soldiers and police, now called 'security forces', were indemnified for any act of violence committed against the local population. Soldiers as well as police had unlimited powers to detain, raid and search; break up meetings and funerals; set up road blocks; impose curfews and seal off any township or village to prevent anyone from entering. Even aircraft would be used in security force 'operations' for surveillance, or to drop propaganda literature as part of a show of force during evictions of rent boycotters, and for actually diving on demonstrations. Townships were put under spotlights to facilitate operations at night.

During this time we have seen the brutal murders of our people by South Africa's 'security forces', vigilantes and hit-squads. People have been displaced by the terror unleashed by these forces. There has also been a vicious disinformation campaign which has been aggravated by restrictions on the free flow of information.

The mobilisation of the army against the black majority showed most clearly that the regime regarded the entire oppressed people as 'insurgents'. They were intent on breaking the spirit of resistance, wiping out the forces of national liberation and creating a political wasteland into which government proxy forces and other co-optable elements would step in. Reports reaching churches and other bodies monitoring repression around the country clearly indicated that after the State of Emergency a wide range of people, regardless of their political involvement, were being terrorised by the forces of so-called law and order.

What emerges clearly from these reports, though, is that the main target of this terror has been the youth and the children. This is not surprising because since 16 June, 1976, the most militant, energetic and courageous fighters against apartheid have been the youth and children. Many are driven by sheer hatred of apartheid to engage daily in a battle with the security forces and all those they regard as enforcing apartheid.

The state therefore concluded that to break the spirit of the community they had to break the spirit of the youth. Not only those formally involved in the organisations of the democratic movement, but all the youth.

Hundreds of reports reached us of apparently random assault, harassment and the shooting of youths in the streets, at school, on the way to shops, at funerals and vigils and so on. A pattern emerged which repeated itself in every part of the country. The attacks weren't simply the actions of overzealous security forces, but were actually part of a deliberate policy of terrorising the youth. Anyone who thinks that it is an exaggeration to talk of a

31

On a Friday, after school, I was walking with my friend when I saw a Combi containing policemen coming towards us. My friend was scared so he ran away. Six police, two whites and four blacks, got out of the Combi. The white policeman knocked me down with his gun and then three of them took me to the street corner. The other three had started chasing my friend in a Combi but they did not catch him. The white policeman and two black policemen then assaulted me with rubber truncheons. They threatened me with a knife. One of the policemen told me to run so that they could shoot me. The Combi with the other police then came back and they threw me in the Combi. They drove to a schoolyard where they assaulted me again. They hit me with rubber truncheons and sjamboks. Then they blindfolded me with a greasy cloth and tied my hands behind my back with my belt.

They put me against a wall and said they were going to shoot me. People had come into the schoolyard and when they saw me against the wall, they started screaming. The police then took the blindfold away and showed me a tyre which they said they were going to put on me and then set me alight. A black policeman said that they had been sent from Port Elizabeth to kill people and that I would be an example for them. But the white policeman said they must stop because the other people in the schoolyard had taken the car registration number. Then they took me to a police station and asked the police there to detain me for 'suspected car theft'. Three days later I was released without being charged for anything.

Statement of a 15-year-old boy who had never been a political activist, cited by Frank Chikane

policy of terror, should consider the testimony of young people.

To intimidate and demoralise the youth, particularly school kids, they introduced curfews, door-to-door raids, shows of force at funerals and meetings. Our children came under heavy attack in schools. At one stage in the emergency schools were occupied by the security forces. School children reported that they were terrorised by the security forces. Soldiers and police interfered in the classes, attacked and shot children in the school grounds, whipped them into classes, etc.

Besides being terrorised at school, on the streets and in their houses, many of them were detained and tortured in ways that have been documented by the Detainees' Parents Support Committee. Many detained children have reported that they were terrorised and assaulted in detention until they 'confessed' to crimes they had not committed. Even the courts have been used as a weapon to terrorise the children. Children themselves who have been victims of security violence are often charged for 'public violence'. If you have been shot, for instance, you are assumed to have been committing a crime. According to the Minister of Law and Order, over 1,100 people were charged with public violence in 1986 alone. What the Minister's figures do not show, however, are the vast numbers of the children who were convicted on false evidence and those who were acquitted or had their charges dropped for lack of evidence. Occasionally the gross injustice of the whole process is exposed, as in the case this month of the 12-year-old boy who had charges of public violence dropped against him. The boy, a standard two pupil from Parys, had spent 11 months in detention under the Emergency Regulations. The State alleged that he had confessed to throwing stones at the car of a township superintendent in June 1986. But the defence lawyer discovered that the said 'confession' had been written in Afrikaans, a language that the boy did not understand. Charges against him and three others were dropped.

It is clear, then, that the use of the state repressive apparatus was built into the 'total strategy' approach. It was meant to silence and suppress those who refused to collaborate with the efforts of the system to maintain white domination in the country. The goal of this strategy of repression therefore is to beat our people into submission, create a political wasteland to enable them to continue with their reforms. In South Africa one does not need to have been violent to face the brutal hand of this system. One just needs to differ with the system, or expose the intention behind these reforms, detect that they are meant to retrench apartheid and retain power in the hands of the white racist minority, to qualify to be brutalised by this system.

For instance, many leaders of the UDF have been in detention under the State of Emergency Regulations for more than a year without any charges proferred against them, but they have not raised their hands or picked up a stone against anyone. What have 'Terror' Lekota, Popo Molefe, Moss Chikane and others in the Delmas Treason trial done except be lamentably peaceful in their struggle to end apartheid in South Africa?

Members of the National Education Crisis Committee (NECC) are now languishing in prison. What have they done except to negotiate with the government to try and resolve the education crisis? The same applies to Eric Molobi, who is the only remaining member of the NECC executive not in detention at present, and has had to be in hiding for almost a year now to avoid being

33

Since the reopening of the school term on 14 July 1986, members of the South African Police and council police have been on the school premises at all times. For me, as a teacher, the very presence of security forces disrupts the teaching programme. My students often ask me why these police are always around, but because of the warnings from the principal I was unable to discuss even these problems with the students in my class . . . During breaktime the security forces bar the gate leading onto the school premises so as to stop anybody leaving the school grounds. As soon as the siren sounds to end break, they immediately proceed to start whipping people into the classrooms. They do not even allow a reasonable time for people to get from the school yard to classes, but they sjambok them to hasten their route to the classroom . . . I have subsequently seen bruises and cuts by these actions on many of my students . . . Pupils are being unlawfully assaulted and abused in an arbitrary fashion without reason. Cases of mass arrests of schoolchildren were reported. In one instance a whole school of 1,200 Soweto schoolchildren were arrested apparently for having left the school ground at a time when the Emergency Restrictions did not allow. The Supreme Court secured their release. I personally had an experience of battling with other ministers to secure the release of primary school children detained with their teachers because they broke the curfew regulations.

From a sworn affidavit by a teacher from the Orange Free State

detained by the apartheid security forces. Did they not talk to government ministers to resolve the education crisis? The only reason I can see in this case is that they did not readily agree with the strategies of the regime and therefore had to be removed from the scene to leave only those black 'faces' which will agree with them in their strategies.

So I am convinced that the regime's demand for the ANC to abandon violence before they can negotiate with them is just a bluff. It is a smokescreen to avoid facing the reality of genuine negotiations which will interfere with the dominant position of whites in this country. Violence is not the issue here – white power is the issue.

I cannot but reject the latest constitutional plan for a powerless advisory council for Africans. The proposed National Statutory Council aims to suppress all democratic patriots of South Africa, leaving the co-optable elements of the black community to participate. If they were genuine about negotiations they would unban the liberation movements, release Mandela and other political prisoners, and let those in exile come back home to all participate in this process.

The regime's strategy of counter-revolution, as articulated lately by Vlok, Malan and others,is, firstly, to engage in generalised terror against our people in the name of crushing revolutionaries and radicals, beat them into submission or remove them from the scene; secondly, to engage in limited economic and political reforms to pacify the people and try to win their 'hearts and minds'; and thirdly, to introduce the so-called new dispensation, in a political vacuum to enable them to secure white power domination. This is the so-called three-phase strategy of counter-revolution the system is committed to and this sequence can be repeated from time to time as it becomes necessary.

This, therefore, is the context and basis for the repression against the children of South Africa. There is very little that can be done to save and protect the brutalised children of South Africa without necessarily removing the apartheid system. The racist apartheid regime is evil and can only survive by murdering hundreds of thousands of defenceless people in South Africa. The determination of the people to be free will force this system to unleash all its powers at the expense of countless lives. If nothing is done we shall soon be talking about millions dead.

Apartheid must be stopped!

I wish to take this opportunity to represent the views and feelings of the majority of the peace-loving South Africans by calling on the international community to put pressure on South Africa to force them to abandon the apartheid system and allow all the people of South Africa to set up a new government based on a new constitution to establish a united, just and non-racial democratic South Africa.

TESTIMONY OF THE CHILDREN

One after another children and youths stepped on to the dais to speak to the conference about personal experiences so painful and terrifying that the listening adults could barely meet each other's eyes to read the impact of what they had heard. Each child spoke to a lawyer who slowly took them through their stories. Only William Modibedi, even though he was accompanied by his mother and a young priest from the DPSC, found himself unable to speak, overcome by fear of what might happen to him when he went back to South Africa.

On the platform the youths were composed, dignified, as they told their stories, their psychological scarring well hidden. The horrifying testimonies of Buras Nhlabathi, Mzimkulu Ngamlana and Naude Moitse printed here, like the earlier one of Moses Madia, are very far from exceptional. In two months of 1985, in just two prisons, Dr Wendy Orr cited prison documents listing 706 detainees who complained of assault or who showed injuries consistent with assault. The four days of Harare could have been filled over and over by personal testimony equally unbearable to hear and record.

William Modibedi

Although William Modibedi, age 12, found it difficult to speak at the conference of his experience, he had previously told it to a lawyer who recorded it in an affidavit. What follows is drawn from a report published in the Johannesburg Star on 11 December 1986.

'William Modibedi is a Kagiso schoolboy of eleven just released from detention. He has few words to describe what it is like inside the cells: when asked to recount his experiences over the two months when he was away from home, he indifferently relates what happened to him. But pressed to be specific, he cries.

'William alleges that he was forced to stand for lengthy periods during interrogation at Roodepoort Police Station, and that the same happened at Krugersdorp Police Station where he was interrogated again.

'He says that in Roodepoort four of his teeth were knocked out by a black policeman during interrogation.

I was later led to a darkened room where a light bulb was switched on and I was forced to stare at its glare. I stared at it until I felt dizzy. Even with the light on, the room somehow remained dim.

On 27 October I was transferred to Krugersdorp Prison, called 'Berg', and two days later I was taken to Krugersdorp Police Station for further interrogation. When I arrived there I was handcuffed and put in leg-irons, and then subjected to electric shocks.

They put a dummy into my mouth, and the dummy had wires connected to it. The wires were connected to a socket in the wall, and when a policeman turned on the switch I experienced a jarring effect. I also felt excruciating pains in my head.

'He said the reason he was being tortured was to force him to sign statements admitting he had attacked three delivery trucks with petrol bombs. He was also forced to incriminate himself concerning an incident of "necklacing".

'"Because of the pain, I signed the statement," he said.

'Some days later he was taken by the police to a mortuary where he was forced to look at dead bodies. This happened on two occasions, once in the morning and the other at night.

'William says that a policeman also pushed him down a flight of stairs.

'His two sisters Elsie (18) and Sophie (15) and brother John (16) are still in detention.

'Elsie was the first to be detained in July, John was picked up some weeks later and William and Sophie were detained together in a dawn raid on their home in October.

'Elsie and John are being held in the Diepkloof Prison, Johannesburg, and Sophie is in Roodepoort.

'A psychiatrist who saw the child said he would not say yet that William's condition was post-traumatic stress syndrome.

'The doctor said, however, that the kind of experiences William had allegedly undergone in prison could have a lasting effect on him. The boy would probably readjust to home life at a faster pace if his detained brother and sisters were released to be with him.

'But there was a possibility William's condition could be adversely affected by the stories he and his siblings exchanged of their experiences in the cells.'

Mzimkulu Ngamlana

Mzimkulu Ngamlana was 18 years old and a member of the Port Elizabeth Youth Congress when he was detained. He left South Africa in August 1986 and now lives in Tanzania.

I went to the funerals of two of my mates – one was shot in the head by police and one in the stomach. They died. The police were at the funeral, taking photos and checking people there. I went home afterwards and stayed inside for three days. Then police came in the house, kicked the door and got in. I was sleeping, with my mother and my sister and my sister's children aged seven and four. It was 5 am. My mother asked them why they had come, but they didn't answer her, they didn't tell us anything. They pushed my mother although she is old. There were more than five men in uniform, they kicked me with their boots. They have my photos. I was afraid.

They kicked me and punched me on the legs and chest. In the police station two of those holding me connected an electric tube on to my leg and switched it on. It was bad, I was shaking. They were asking me questions about my friends. My mother brought me food but they ate it. In the prison I was in solitary confinement. I was crying and just sitting. After three weeks I was released. My ears were bleeding and my head hurt.

After my release I could not stand it. Every night I would hear gun shots, you cannot learn or do anything.

Naude Moitse

Naude Moitse now lives in Tanzania. He was brought up in Alexandra and attended Minerva High School where he was in form 5 in 1984. His testimony to the conference covered two years from the time he was 19 years old. As well as being involved in COSAS, he was active in community organisation, and in organising funerals of people killed by police.

Around March or April I was involved in COSAS in the school boycotts. We used to hold meetings at school during the boycott, which had been going for some days. On our way home a group of us – about five – were stopped by plainclothes police in private cars. They came from John Vorster Square. They told us they were from Security Branch. They wanted our names and where we lived. We gave them the information. They forced us into the cars, took us to Wynberg police station. They took photographs, and hung them round our necks. They did not hit us. They only held us for a few hours. They said they knew we were involved in boycotts. They took us home.

We continued with the boycott. I was detained again around September 1984. There was a parents' meeting organised by the puppet Town Council. It was to discuss the boycott, but they didn't consult the students. We went to the meeting place at Nobuhle Hall. We distributed a COSAS pamphlet explaining the boycott and what we thought parents should do. The police charged us with batons and whips. They fired birdshot. They caught some of us. They kicked me in the genitals. It was very painful. They handcuffed me and took me to Wynberg Police Station.

The SAP interrogated us. They accused us of stone-throwing and public violence. One policeman came and said he knew persons who threw stones and said it wasn't me. We were distributing pamphlets which were quite legal. We were kept for the whole day. Security Branch came to interrogate us. I was alone in a cell with a security policeman. He threatened me. Late in the evening I was released.

After the Emergency in July 1985, police kept coming in large numbers turning our home upside down at 3 or 4 in the morning. They told my parents they would kill me if they found me. When the Emergency was declared I had left home. I was active in COSAS.

I had an appointment with a comrade who was just released. We wanted to discuss reviving structures. He turned out to be an informer who had police with him. Police pointed a gun and said if I move they will shoot. They handcuffed me to my leg and bundled me in a car. Also there were plainclothes police. I knew them before, Chauke (a black man) and Kees (a white) from John Vorster Square. They said that they were aware of my activities and they know that I have a link with the ANC.

They took me to the office in Wynberg. It was a Friday. They took particulars and photos. They threatened me they would either kill me or keep me in jail for a long time. They accused me of links with ANC. I said I was only involved in student activities.

Well, they wanted me to tell them about my links with the ANC. They suspected that I had been outside for training. I told them that I've never been involved in such a thing. And they were worried that they were looking for quite a long time, they couldn't find me. So I might have been a trained person, knowing how to go about fooling the police and all that – they were worried about such things. So I just told them I've been around the township. I was aware they were looking for me, but I had to run away, because of the way they behaved, the way that I understand that they came in large numbers with rifles, gave me the impression that I might be killed. That's why I wouldn't appear, I mean, on the scene. So I had to go into hiding.

At 2pm they took me to John Vorster Square. I was made to stand up for more than 12 hours by Mike Fortuin, a well-known police officer. When I fell they picked me up, kicked me on my body. They didn't want to leave marks. They gave me no food. I had only water to drink. At 2am they took me to a cell. I had to sleep on a concrete floor wearing a T-shirt and jeans.

At around 8 they gave me soft porridge and bread. It was the first I'd had to eat since they arrested me.

I kept on telling the same things. The interrogator came again after breakfast. He told me I must be ready for a long detention. He said they'd keep me until they were satisfied. He left me. It was Saturday. He said he'd see me on Monday. I was kept in the cell. There was a TV monitor on the ceiling. The food was very little but edible. Monday a policeman came at around 2. I was taken to another floor. Another 12 hours standing upright. There was no food, only water. I was exhausted. I was kicked again. I still said no more.

There were five policemen, one of them I remember well because he was the one interrogating me. They were asking me questions about when was I outside the country, to see if I was a trained person. I had the impression I might be killed, – they would say, 'you see this window . . . '

After that interrogation, there was another the following day, just the same. He said he'd give me a whole month. There was a Bible in the cell. They came and took the Bible away. I was in solitary confinement for three months. The light was always on, the window was very, very far up, there was no privacy, they were always watching me. They told me they had all the time. I was kept alone. I did not know what would happen to me. But the thing always tormenting me during my detention was the cries of kids, kids in other cells I could only hear. After three to four weeks they resumed the interrogation. I went four to five days without bathing. Warders would open and bang door at night to wake me up. They released me on 21 March 1986, when the Emergency had been lifted.

Afterwards they kept harassing my parents at home, coming with hippos, army trucks, armoured cars.

I was detained again for 14 days in May 1986. I was stopped by soldiers in the township. They searched the car – there were four

40

of us. They checked the car registration. They were in army trucks. They left us, then they came again. There were two hippos and trucks. They pointed guns, and bundled us into hippos. Then they beat us with gun barrels – calling us terrorists.

At Morningside Prison, Sandton, Fortuin again interrogated me. This time they threatened to hand us to vigilantes. They took a tyre and threatened to necklace one of us. I was in isolation for 14 days. The food was bad – plain pap. Some fruit was brought in from outside. My parents were not allowed to visit me. My parents told me that they came several times with food parcels, with money, but they were told that I was okay, that there was nothing wrong with me, they shouldn't worry. So they were not allowed to see me or to give me anything.

I was charged with breach of restrictions on a funeral and taken to court. The lawyer told us the charge was dropped. I was released. But the harassment continued. After the Emergency came into force they put out a pamphlet with our photos – wanted by security police. They were distributed all over townships, offering reward. I left the country.

Buras Nhlabathi

Buras Nhlabathi was 17 when he was detained. He was President of the Tembisa Youth Congress, as well as active on residents' committees in the area in which he lived (sectional committee and street committee). When he was detained in October 1986 residents in the area were refusing to pay rents they could not afford to the councils imposed by the government. Students were engaged in a school boycott. Buras is now at the ANC's Solomon Mahlangu Freedom College in Tanzania.

I was president of the local student congress and secretary of the Sectional Committee. We were politicising people – explaining why they should not pay rent, for instance, and issuing pamphlets. We called for the enemy to be ignored and this means that people's local problems and matters are brought to the sectional committee and we, the street committee, have to deal with them. We tried to form a people's court.

I had not been living at home because I had actually been running away from the police. I had been staying with four others in a house about half a kilometre from my home.

I was arrested at 3.30 in the morning on 8 October 1986. There were four whites and two blacks and South African Defence Force personnel surrounding the house.

41

And then when they entered the house – actually we were sleeping being four in that house, because all the members of the executive were highly wanted by that time. So we used to sleep together so that we can trust each other, I mean if we are sleeping together we know that nobody would come and point at you because you are all together in the one house.

So then, when they came inside the house they asked me my name firstly, and then I told them my name and then they said I'm the right person whom they are looking for. Then from there I was beaten up for something like 45 minutes inside the house. I was beaten with fists, kicked and hit with the butt of a gun for about 45 minutes. They were seeking information about the four comrades I studied with.

They wanted to take me from the house naked, but I took a shirt, trousers and shoes.

I was thrown in a van. I thought I was being taken to a police station, but I was taken to my home. I saw the whole section where I was living was surrounded. They left me in the van and came out with my older brother. Altogether they arrested 12 others from my committee. We were all taken to Tembisa Police Station. It was raining and we were left outside. We were then separated. At about 5 am I was taken into an interrogation room.

And then they started interrogating me, beating me up for something like 5 hours because, I remember very well, they started at 5 am, until 10 am in the morning. They asked me if I know something about the African National Congress, and about the campaign which maybe the Student Congress is planning and again about other members whom they can't find. Posters of banned organisations were shown to me that had been displayed in schools and around the community. I was questioned about them – who put them up, where they were printed. When I refused to answer, I was beaten. They said as I was president I was influencing other students in the boycott.

I was at Tembisa Police Station for one day. I was beaten and given electric shocks from handcuffs. Then I was also taken to a room where there are bright search lights and by the time I came out of that room I couldn't see nothing and I felt like my mind was tired and they started beating me up and then the only thing I remember is that when I started being normal, you know, I mean my mind now working normally, I realised that I was injured in my body. All my comrades were released. I stood firm, preferring to die.

During the first day at Tembisa Police Station, even my mother was refused permission to see me and actually didn't have any

42

confirmation that I was detained. She got the information after my brother was released because he was released the same day and then he told my mother that I am also there.

On the second day, I was taken to Kempton Park Police Station, I was given electric shocks. I was stripped and put in a rubber suit from head to foot. A dummy was put in my mouth so I could not scream. There was no air. They switched the plug on. My muscles pumping hard, no signs on my body. I couldn't see anything.

When they switched the plug off they took the dummy out and said I should speak. When I refused, they put the dummy back and switched on again. After a long time they stopped. I was stripped and put into a refrigerated room naked. I was left there. In the fridge it was also something like 30 minutes. Then they brought me out again and put me back in the electric shock suit. I was then taken into another interrogation room. My hands, feet and head were tied around a pole and bright search lights turned on. I could not remove my head from those search lights. And then they brightened them straight into my face. I felt my mind go dead. I couldn't see. I cannot even read at this present juncture. I was dizzy. I was beaten again for the whole day. I have scars on my right hip, in my head and on my back.

I was then taken to Modderbee Prison. I was given no medical treatment on arrival. I was given ice cubes for my swollen face. I was in prison for three months. I spent two weeks in solitary confinement. Sometimes I would be there for two weeks and then they took me out again. They were changing. It depends, because if they've detained somebody from the membership of the organisation and maybe if that somebody has revealed certain information about me to them, then they came to my cell telling me, 'So-and-so has told us about you.' And then, 'It seems you were telling us the wrong information and you are not prepared to say the right information.' So then they took me back to the solitary confinement.

Maybe after two weeks then they would take me out again and if they detain somebody I would go back again. I was beaten in prison, but only with fists. After my release I was to report at 7 am and 7 pm at the police station. I didn't. I spent five months in hiding after my release before leaving. I could not attend school. My family do not know where I am.

'Kids who never made Harare'

Shortly after the Harare Conference the weekly newspaper South *published reports on 22 October of what had happened to four*

43

children in the Western Cape during the previous two years. The reports are reproduced here.

Themba Ivan Nkalashe

When Themba Ivan Nkalashe left home on 18 November 1985 he thought it would be just another day on the beach with his friends. Little did he know that he would end up at Victor Verster Prison in Paarl under the Emergency Regulations. Themba, then 13, was one of a group of youths arrested near Philippi when they returned from Mnandi Beach. He was one of the youngest children to be detained under the 1985 State of Emergency.

> I was returning home with some of my friends when we saw some boys throwing stones at the trains near Kapteinsklip Station in Mitchells Plain. We decided to go to the next station. We saw some boys stoning a truck. They were all running but we were walking. The police came and arrested us. At the Mitchells Plain Police Station they asked me why the boys attacked shops, cars and trains.

Themba was kept at the police station for three days before he was taken to Victor Verster Prison where he was held for another five days.

> I was not questioned once at Victor Verster even though some of the other boys arrested at the same time were questioned. We were about eight or nine in the cell and had to sleep on mats on the floor. On the day of my release I was taken to the Athlone Police Station and told to walk home to Guguletu.

He said his family was not officially informed of his detention.

> Someone who saw me being arrested told them. They tried to visit me at Mitchells Plain but were refused permission. I still feel angry at being detained. I did not do anything. Even today I am still scared to go to Mnandi Beach.

He was not charged on his release.

Mongesi Gwabeni

Mongesi Gwabeni is still suffering from the effects of his two

44

weeks in detention in November 1985. He missed his Standard Three final examination at Lehlohonolo Combined Primary School in Section 3, Guguletu, that year because of his detention. He is now trying to catch up by attending evening classes at X3 High School in New Crossroads where he is doing Standard Four. He has also developed chest problems and spent six weeks in hospital. He said he had never had chest problems before his detention.

Mongesi, who was 17 at the time, was one of the boys detained on their way home after a day at Mnandi Beach.

My friends and I wanted to take a train from Kapteins-klip station to Guguletu but were chased away by the police. We decided to walk home. On the way we saw some other boys throwing stones.

At Philippi station the police came and we ran away because we had heard that they took children. I ran into an auntie's garden and started to water the garden with a hosepipe. Unfortunately, I did not see that a police-man had followed me so I was arrested.

When we arrived at Mitchells Plain police station there were about 50 children. After three days, they took us to Victor Verster Prison in Paarl. I stayed there for 14 days. I was called in for questioning every day. On the day of my release, I was dropped in Bellville and had to take a taxi home. I was not charged with any offence.

His mother, Mrs Joyce Gwabeni, said she was refused permission to see her son at Mitchells Plain:

They told me I could not see him because he had thrown stones. I did not see him until he was released. He was sick when he came home. He was only home for three days when we took him to Brooklyn Chest Hospital where he spent six weeks.

'Because of my detention and the time I spent in hospital, I was unable to write exams and had to repeat the year,' Mongesi said. He said he had to sleep on thin mats on the floor at Victor Verster.

We had many complaints, like the food which was not nice. The food was even worse at the Mitchells Plain Police Station where we received only bread and soup.

45

Ben Makhenkwe

Ben Makhenkwe Sono has not slept on a bed since his detention in December last year. Ben, 19 at the time of his detention, claimed he has had severe headaches and backache problems.

> I am now unable to sleep on a soft bed because it might damage my back more. I have to sleep on a mat on the floor. I never had these kind of problems before.

Ben said he was arrested at KTC at the beginning of December. He did not know of any fighting or unrest in the area at the time.

> I was taken to Manenberg Police Station where the police accused me of being a qabane (comrade). I told them I'm a rastaman and I stand for peace. I was held at Manenberg for two weeks and released shortly before Christmas.
>
> I was not allowed visitors at the police station. I was given a mat and two blankets and had to sleep on a concrete floor. For the two weeks I only drank water because as a rastaman I do not eat bread and meat. I had no clean clothes and had to wear the clothes in which I was arrested throughout my period in detention.

Ben said he was arrested again in June: 'The police drove around with me and dropped me at Old Crossroads. They again accused me of being a comrade.'

He has a certificate from Dr R Thompson, the Medical officer at Conradie Hospital, confirming that he had been treated for head injuries on 26 June.

Ashraf Abrahams

The small body of Ashraf Abrahams is covererd by marks left by birdshot and bullet wounds. The marks serve as a grim reminder of 15 October 1985 – the day police, hidden in crates on the back of a truck, shot and killed three youths in what has become known as the 'Trojan Horse' shootings.

Ashraf, then 7 years old, and about 20 of his relatives, mainly children, were at a house in Thornton Road, Belgravia, opposite the scene of the shootings. One of the boys killed that day, Shaun Magmoet, ran into the house and fell dead on a bed. The other boys killed that day were Michael Miranda and Jonathan Claasen. Almost all the children in the house had to be treated in hospital after heavily-armed police stormed and kicked down the door of the house. 'It was like Blood River. It still sends shivers down my spine every time I think of what happened,' said Ashraf's mother, Mrs Amiena Abrahams.

There was an air of expectation and nervousness in the busy house on the eve of the second anniversary of the shootings last week. As children streamed in and out of the house, the adults seemed visibly concerned that what happened two years ago could be repeated. 'Last year this time, we became very nervous every time the police drove past. We expected them to come in and harass us,' said Mrs Abrahams.

Ashraf seemed nervous and hesitant to speak about what happened two years ago, when street battles between youths and the police took place daily. 'My mother had come to fetch me at the madressa. I was sitting on the bed, talking to the other children.' He paused and his mother continued:

> I went to look through the kitchen window to see what was going on outside. Suddenly I heard shots.
> There was compete chaos after that as the police stormed into the house. The children were screaming and there was blood everywhere.
> Ashraf had to be rushed to hospital. I could not see how much he was bleeding because he wore a maroon and black jersey. I only realised how serious it was when the doctor told me he was very lucky to be alive.

Ashraf stayed in hospital for a month. He missed his Sub A examinations and had to repeat the year at Heatherdale Primary School, in Belgravia Road. He is now in Sub B. 'Since that time Ashraf has not been as active. He developed asthma and gets tired very quickly. He is still on medication,' his mother said.

Ashraf's cousin, Ismaiel Ryklief, who was 12 at the time of the shootings, said he was the last person 'Trojan Horse' victim Shaun Magmoet spoke to before he died:

> He was lying on the bed and tried to mumble something to me. And then he died. I will never forget that day. We were watching videos with some friends. They wanted to go home so we went outside. We saw this truck going past and the police jumping out of boxes on the back. We ran inside and my aunt locked the door. The police first stood at the windows, and then kicked down the door and came inside.

Shaun ran into the house with us and fell dead on the bed.

The police wanted to arrest me, but they left me after the others protested. I had wounds on my one finger on my right hand, my right thigh, and my back. I was treated at Groote Schuur Hospital and the Red Cross before being discharged that same night. It feels like I still have birdshot inside me. I used to run for the school, but I can't anymore. I have also given up soccer and cricket.

Ismaiel was in Standard Three at the time of the shootings. He is now in Standard Five at Sunnyside Primary School. The parents of the boys who died refused to speak to the press.

LAW AND ORDER WITHOUT LAW

The story of Moses Madia comes to the outside world only in an affidavit to his lawyer. Thousands of such affidavits in which repression's victims have told their own stories in the most direct indictment of the South African state have been taken by South African lawyers and publicised by them rather than by journalists who have been generally less prepared to push against the state's increasing powers under the State of Emergency. The few in the legal profession who have chosen to mount challenges to the apartheid regime on behalf of the otherwise powerless have been an important resource to the democratic movement's resistance for years. They have become even more important as the state's powers of repression have grown and as one lawyer put it, 'the judiciary has chosen sides with the executive'.

A glimpse of the conditions in which 'law' is practised in South Africa came, for instance, when one of the Harare participants told of sitting in a car with his client, taking down a statement, while three truck loads of soldiers drove back and forth past them, using loud hailers to shout, 'we'll come and get you when your lawyers have gone'.

South African Legal Framework and the Child

Conference background papers and the presentations of various lawyers, particularly Advocate Langa and Professor David McQuoid-Mason, gave an exhaustive review of the position of children under South African law. Those contributions form the basis of this overview of how the law forms an integral part of the repression of children, sanctioning arbitrary detention and independent monitoring of the treatment of children by the courts themselves.

South African law recognises the special needs of children at a number of points. The common law presumes that children under 14 are not capable of criminal intent unless the oppposite can be proved. The Child Care Act of 1983 prohibits the ill-treatment and neglect of children. The Prisons Act of 1959 provides that children should be held separately from adults. The Criminal Procedure Act of 1977 requires that the trials of children (persons under 18 years of age) be held in camera, that children may be assisted in their defence by their parents and that the court may use various alternatives to imprisonment or whipping (reformatories, places of safety, probation).

However, studies by academics and lawyers, including conference background papers by Pius Langa and David McQuoid-Mason, have pointed out that, apart from the fact that 'security legislation' overrides these protections, they are anyway rendered illusory in practice.

- Parents are often not notified of their children's trials. In any event most parents would not be familiar enough with legal procedures to conduct a defence on behalf of their child.
- There is no obligation on the part of the state to provide a legal representative for children and accordingly many children even as young as 9 or 10 are convicted without legal representation.
- Because of the lack of actual facilities that could serve as alternatives to imprisonment or whipping, the latter is the most common punishment meted out. In political cases unrepresented children are being sentenced to lengthy terms of imprisonment.
- Children, black children especially, are held for long periods in custody prior to trial. In many cases bail pending the trial is refused. At the end of the trial, particularly those concerning protest-related offences, the overwhelming majority, over 80 per cent, of children will have been acquitted or have had the charges withdrawn. By this time they will have spent anything from 3 to 12 months as awaiting-trial prisoners. This is punishment by process.
- The conditions under which children are held in police stations and prisons are far from satisfactory. Apart from the allegations of unlawful assault, the law itself does not require the authorities to provide any kind of special support for children. For example, children and their parents have had to struggle for three years to be allowed study 'privileges'.
- The secrecy (in camera) provisions relating to the trials of juveniles work against those charged with 'unrest-related' offences isolating the accused from his/her community.

Security Legislation and Children

The worst allegations of abuse of children, torture and assault concern their treatment while being held under powers allowing detention without trial. The most prominent feature of such detention, whether under the legal regime established by the

Public Safety Act of 1953 (the 'Emergency Regulations') or the Internal Security Act of 1982, is that it is within a framework of laws which prevent access to information about a detainee. At the same time they grant wide, almost unconstrained powers to police officials, notably interrogators. Since the introduction in 1963 of the detention without trial provisions over 60 persons have died in detention. Furthermore, countless persons have made confessions, or been convicted on the basis of confessions made in indefinite solitary confinement in terms of Section 29 of the Internal Security Act or its predecessor Section 6 of the Terrorism Act. For this reason detention without trial has been referred to as the 'confession factory'. The laws which allow for detention are as follows:

- **Internal Security Act of 1982**   This allows the detention – of adults or children – under various circumstances: Section 29 allows indefinite detention in solitary confinement for the purposes of interrogation; Section 31 allows detention of potential state witnesses. In each of these cases people can be held incommunicado and no-one has the right to publish their names without official authorisation. Sections 50 and 50a allow detention 'in situations of unrest', the former for up to 14 days, the latter after the State President has declared an area to be an unrest area, for 180 days. These clauses do not authorise interrogation. Children are not granted any special protection in terms of this legislation, either physically, mentally or legally. Similar laws and powers exist in the bantustans declared 'independent', through the Bophuthatswana Internal Security Act, the Transkei Public Security Act, the Ciskei National Security Act and the Venda Maintenance of Law and Order Act.

  Section 29 is a refined version of Section 6 of the Terrorism Act. The refinement, added after the revelations of abuse of detainees which followed the deaths of Steve Biko and Neil Aggett, consists of allowing certain state officials access to detainees. Critics have correctly pointed out that the system remains a closed one. The officials report only to other government officials. Detainees report that while in Section 29 detention they feel at the mercy of their interrogators and that they can be assaulted without anyone ever knowing.

- **Public Safety Act of 1953**   This allows the State President to declare an emergency and to impose Emergency Regulations for up to one year. This power was used in July 1985, and then again in June 1986 and June 1987, to give the police, army and prisons service the power to detain any one without warrant and hold them in detention. An initial period of detention (currently 30 days) can be extended indefinitely until the emergency ends. Children are given no special protection under the Emergency Regulations and the Child Care Act cannot protect them. It was recently submitted in court that Parliament having shown it's concern for children by means of the Child Care Act, could not have intended that the State President in exercising powers under the Public Safety Act, should permit the arrest and detention of young children by any soldier, policeman, or prison official. The court held, however, that the State President did have such power.

A report by the Detainees' Parents Support Committee (DPSC) in November last year revealed how bad the conditions were under which children were being detained during the emergency. Anything up to 40 people were commonly being held together in cells which were frequently filthy and cold. Other reports have indicated that the children are sometimes held with adult prisoners. Children have no right of access to parents or lawyers – nor do parents have right of access to their children. Without legal assistance it is nearly impossible for ordinary parents to trace a missing child to a specific detention centre. There is no legal obligation placed upon the police to notify a parent that his/her child is in detention. Restrictions on publishing the names of detainees prevent parents from campaigning for the release of their children. Apart from the detention of children, the violence perpetrated on them in the townships and streets cannot be reported because the Emergency Regulations prohibit the reporting of 'unrest-related' events.

The courts are limited in their ability to intervene and adjudicate on police abuses because the Emergency Regulations give a wide (subjective) discretion to police officials; limit the right of the courts to judge the validity of police actions or orders; and finally, grant the police an indemnity against civil or criminal proceedings which may be brought against them for unlawful acts which they did in 'good faith'.

Why does the state prefer to detain people, especially under the provisions of the Emergency Regulations? Whereas the Internal Security Act requires a senior commissioned police officer to authorise the detention of a child, the Emergency Regulations grant that power to any member, even a raw recruit of the SAP or SADF. Furthermore, the Internal Security Act requires the arresting officer to have 'reasonable' grounds for the detention, whereas the Emergency Regulations do not require that the grounds for the detention be reasonable nor even founded on a correct factual basis. The courts have not required the detaining officer to exercise any distinctive or more onerous discretion when detaining a child as opposed to an adult. Indeed such a suggestion was disregarded by the Supreme Court in *Makhajane v Minister of Law and Order (Witwatersrand Local Division 29.8.86 unreported).*

Pius Langa commented at the end of his paper that the most fearful consequence of the way in which the Emergency Regulations affect South African society is that 'a society is being created whose children have become brutalised. What could be more calculated to make the children lose their sense of balance. It is obvious that what is rendering this country ungovernable are the seeds of wrath planted and nurtured by inhuman laws.'

Recalling a graffiti slogan in Cape Town which reads 'Children must be seen and not HURT', Pius Langa observed:

in my country it seems children are sought out and hurt. Only concerted action by all concerned people and governments will stop this war. There is a new slogan popular amongst children: 'Freedom or Death!' It is a chilling reminder of our urgent responsibility to see to it that South Africa's children enjoy the freedom they are entitled to, and not the death which so pervasively threatens them.

Strategies of Repression

Nicholas Haysom, a practising attorney and academic at the Centre for Applied Legal Studies of the University of Witwatersrand. He has written on repression in the bantustans and on the right-wing vigilante phenomenon.

The increasing scale and intensity of internal and external resistance to apartheid has brought the 'security forces' to the centre of the political stage in South Africa.

The widespread resistance to apartheid institutions throughout rural and urban South Africa surfaced on 3 September 1984 in townships of the industrial heartland of South Africa. The scale of unrest was considered both by officials of the government and apartheid's critics as more extensive than the Soweto students' rebellion of 1976.

The revolt began as a series of demonstrations in these townships. Several factors had converged explosively: the rising cost of living; the deterioration of living standards of township residents whose homes border grotesquely on affluent white suburbs; the imposition of rental and other service charges by community councils – bodies which are seen to be unrepresentative at best and self-serving at worst, and the continuing crisis in black education.

The unrest spread firstly to townships in the Eastern Cape and thereafter to rural areas in 'white' South Africa and the urban areas of the Western Cape and Natal.

In response the police developed harsh, maximum-force policing practices. On 23 October and 5 November 1984 police called upon the assistance of troops in cordoning-off certain townships in the Transvaal and conducting door-to-door searches. The police found it increasingly difficult to contain the unrest and restore matters to what they had been. In one area it was an educational boycott, in another a labour strike, in yet another demonstrations and attacks on the government-supported black municipal authorities.

The authorities decided on a harsh policing option in place of a political solution to the crisis. By 21 November 1984, 130 people had died, mostly at the hands of the police. Police sought and were given even greater powers. In 1985, in 1986 and in 1987 the government declared a State of Emergency and promulgated regulations which gave the police extra-ordinary powers, executive and legislative, in order to cope with the unrest.

How draconian this was can be gauged from a comparison with the powers the authorities possessed prior to the State of Emergency. In all but name they are emergency powers: powers to ban meetings, persons, organisations and literature without notice or a hearing. For over ten years, since 1976, all outdoor gatherings of more than two people have been prohibited in terms of the Internal Security Act.

The most notorious power, to hold indefinitely for interrogation in solitary confinement without any charges, without legal access, has led to the death of over 60 suspects in detention. Large numbers of persons had been detained under these provisions by 1984 and many were subjected to systematic torture, the methods of which included shock, suffocation and assault.

The State of Emergency conferred upon that regime of law an element of normality. Human rights lawyers questioned why it was necessary for the police to be given extra powers. If you look at the powers it is clear that the State of Emergency had a most disturbing and sinister objective.

The first feature is substantially to increase police powers,

54

granting them the widest possible power to detain and arrest by extending this power to raw recruits.

In addition, Divisional Police Commissioners were given powers to govern whole regions simply by decree. These powers have been described as dictatorial and this is not an overstatement. A scrutiny of the orders will reveal that orders have been used to prohibit attendance at funerals, church gatherings, attendance at carol services, to prohibit the wearing of buttons, T-shirts, entry to and from residential areas, to impose curfews, to prevent loitering in public areas, to prevent discussion of certain topics, to order the attendance or prohibit the attendance at schools or other institutions.

The second distinctive feature was to exclude legal process and legal supervision from the exercise of emergency powers. The regulations contained an ouster clause which excludes the courts from exercising jurisdiction over members of the security forces or setting aside orders, regulations or actions made or taken in terms of the State of Emergency. It also gave members of the security force indemnity against their unlawful actions. Furthermore, the regulations cut off access to detainees by attorneys, preventing any monitoring of the conditions and treatment of detainees. Finally, the regulations sought to frame the powers of the security forces in the form of the broadest discretion, avoiding accountability to precise legal standards and procedure. This is a prescription for law and order without law.

The third feature of the Emergency Regulations – and it operates closely with the others – is that the regulations sought to exclude a broader public monitoring of police conduct by a ban on information about unrest events and the photographing and reporting of police conduct. The provisions were so broad and so obscure that many journalists were paralysed not only by the sweep of the regulations, but also by their inscrutability.

All this is a prescription for unsupervised and unaccountable behaviour: unaccountable behaviour by forces vested with substantial executive powers and armed with an array of violent weapons. The security forces had requested and were given permission to use force unconstrained by limits, a capacity to act in the grey area between legality and illegality – a process of pacification by war.

Both before and during the State of Emergency the police liberally used their wide powers to detain people. By 1987 20,000 people had been detained, many of them belonging to youth organisations, trade unions and political organisations. While on the one hand the police sought to neutralise popular organisations

E was walking in the street with some friends. He was a member of both the local Youth Congress and the local Young Christian Students Society. Both these are affiliated to the UDF. Two of the young boys in the group were shot at from a car in which there were white police. One of them was able to run away but E was shot in the back and fell down. One of these men, or maybe more, got out of the car and came to where he was lying. Then he got back into the car.

His family was then called and they took him to the clinic. The family has been told that the bullet is in E's spinal cord and cannot be removed yet.

An account of an attack on a 15-year-old youth activist, cited by the DPSC

such as municipal, youth and labour organisations, by detaining and holding leadership figures, it also embarked on a campaign of mass warehousing of youths. By 1987, 40 per cent of detainees were estimated to be children.

Allegations of assault on detainees have persisted since the inception of the State of Emergency. Since attorneys were granted access to detainees, as a result of court action, the pattern of assaults has diminished but not been eradicated.

The determination of the police to contain the spreading unrest found its effect in what became clinically known as the daily death rate. A typical pattern of violence involved the shooting of a demonstrator in a march, followed by a funeral attendance which was prohibited and, in the ensuing confrontation between mourners and the police, further fatalities which led to further funerals which led to further fatalities.

It appears that the South African police are not trained, equipped or willing to handle crowd control in a humanitarian fashion. Young men riding Casspirs act as judges and execution-ers, deciding whether a child throwing a stone should get a clip round the ear or the death penalty. By 1987 1,000 people had died during protest-related incidents: it was estimated that the majority had died at the hands of the police. As the Bureau for Information was quick to point out, large numbers of persons had also died at the hands of township residents in what they referred to as 'black-on-black violence'. What the Department of Information did not point out was that those persons who had been killed by the police had frequently been killed in circumstances which did not warrant the use of deathly force. Dr Du Flou, Registrar at the University of Cape Town's Department of Forensic Medicine, studied the results of post mortems conducted on the victims of police action. His report claimed that 50 per cent of persons shot by the police had been shot in the back and another 11.6 had wounds in their sides, suggesting that they had turned to run as police opened fire. Twelve per cent of the victims were less than 15 years old – the youngest was seven.

There have now been several instances in which the conduct of the police in the course of township patrols has come under judicial scrutiny. To deal with only one: on 21 March 1985 mourners were walking from one black township to another to attend a funeral. They were confronted by police in armoured vehicles who opened fire with SSG shot guns. SSG shot penetrates metal plates at 30 paces and spreads one metre in thirty. In the course of one savage volley 20 persons were killed and another 43 were injured. The crowd was unarmed. Nineteen of the 20 were shot in the back or the side. In the inquiry into the incident it transpired that the police had not been equipped with non-lethal forms of crowd control such as birdshot, teargas or rubber bullets, and had instead been instructed not to use such equipment, because, as one officer testified at the inquiry, 'it did not immobilise demonstrators'.

There have been numerous similar incidents since the 1984 civil revolt, of which the better known are those that took place at Winterveld, Mamelodi, Soweto, Kabokweni. But the most notorious practice to have emerged recently is that of the Trojan horse. In the first and most publicised of such incidents, police disguised themselves in boxes on the back of a truck and when a few youths began stoning the truck the police jumped out of the boxes and opened fire with lethal weapons, killing three people, including an occupant of a nearby house.

Such incidents, even in South African law, must constitute little short of murder.

More recently, the Supreme Court has had occasion to condemn the conduct of police who were responsible for the killing of black township residents and has commented particularly on their inadequate training and their 'shoot-first' policy. The criticism directed at the police for the use of lethal weapons in the course of crowd control has also been extended to the use of potentially non-lethal weapons, or in the arrest of activists.

Bantustan police are increasingly prominent in human rights violations in South Africa. Yet many of the abuses taking place in South Africa, such as those emanating from Kwazulu, Kwandebele, Ciskei, Transkei and Bophuthatswana are largely ignored by the media.

One incident that has happened very recently shows in graphic detail what we are talking about. I'm especially concerned that many Western countries support a certain organisation in Natal – Inkatha – and its leader because they believe it's a peaceful organisation and the leader is for peace. I just want to give you an example how we experience Inkatha in another light. All the organisations who do support Inkatha should please re-examine the cause they are supporting.

I'm just going to relate one incident of one family. I'm not naming them. In July this family of a trade unionist had a petrol bomb thrown into the house. It hit the 11-year-old son and badly burnt him – he spent quite a time in hospital and is scarred for life. One son, who is also a political activist, went to report the incident and was taken in on the charge of instigation and released a few days later. The same son was detained in August by police but before they took him into their van they allowed UWUSA people, Inkatha trade unionists, to bash him up thoroughly. Then they took him to the police station and released him a few hours later, from where he came to us and we took him to hospital where he was X-rayed for a fractured jaw.

This same family's daughter was killed in late August, coming on the way home from school. One of the alleged killers is the school guard who is a member of Inkatha. On that very same Saturday rumours were spread that the house was going to be burnt down on Saturday night, so very many of the comrades and activists came to help this family and defend them. Instead of Inkatha, the police pitched up and detained 29 young people at that house. They had with them some mysterious bottles of petrol.

On that Sunday night when everybody was in detention, the vigilantes did come and fulfil their promise – they set the house on fire. The mother fled with her grandchild on her back and holding the scarred boy by the hand into the dark. The father – they lost touch with the father. When the sun rose the next morning she went to see what had happened. She found her husband dead at the neighbour's house. The neighbours had also fled and the house was in total ashes.

Monica Wittenburg, a member of the Pietermaritzburg Crisis Committee, part of the network of community-based organisations set up to cope with the effects of the State of Emergency

The South African police's attempt to restore law and order in the townships was essentially a defensive one, in that it was confined to the protection of the targets of community rage, disruption of community organisation and detention of community leaders. By mid-1985 it was clear that policing on its own was having little impact upon the main currents of township politics and was in itself insufficient to restore the community councillors to a position where they could work for the state.

In the latter part of 1985 a new pattern of extra-legal violence emerged in the townships. The authors of the violence came to be known as vigilantes and their targets were the same as those of the security forces – anti-apartheid or popular organisations. In the bantustans the vigilantes enjoyed overt state sponsorship and in the urban areas the motivation and composition of the vigilante groups varied, but in general the vigilantes were grouped around conservative sections of the community. In a survey of vigilante groups throughout the country, it was noted that in all the areas where vigilantes had emerged such groups had enjoyed at least a licence to operate provided by the police or the defence force. In some cases the vigilantes enjoyed open and direct support from the police, but for the vigilantes to be successful it was not necessary for them to be given such overt support: simple police lethargy or reluctance to curb the vigilante violence was sufficient to leave victims vulnerable to potentially fatal attacks and powerless to defend themselves. The various vigilante groupings emerged at approximately the same time and verified police encouragement of vigilante formation in Crossroads and Queenstown is suggestive of a more co-ordinated strategy.

The effect of the vigilante groups is to support the South African police in its attempts to break the back of township-based resistance. Firstly, the violence could be categorised by the government as 'black-on-black violence'. Secondly, there was little or no police visibility in the perpetration of the violence and it gave credence to government claims that vigorous and harsh policing was necessary to protect black township residents from themselves. Thirdly, the vigilante activities proved effective: vigilantes were able to target groups or individuals in a way in which military or police patrolling was unable to do. Fourthly, the level of violence and terror which the vigilantes operating outside the law were able to perpetrate had a much more devastating impact. Communities which had continued to support their civic associations and popular leaders throughout the State of Emergency and despite detentions lost cohesion and direction after the emergence of vigilantes. In some cases civic and youth leaders simply fled the area, abandoning their organisations and communities.

- On the night of 21 December 1985 an 11-year-old boy was spending the night with a friend when a number of men, including three community councillors, entered the house and sjambokked the boy so badly that he bled through his white vest. The police refused to pursue charges when his mother reported the assault.

- In May 1985 a Thabong youth, David Mabinyane, was stopped by a group of pakatis, a vigilante group making open use of the municipal authorities' facilities. He was beaten so badly with sjamboks that he died. After his beating he was taken, significantly, to the police station by the vigilantes and left there. This incident occurred when the pakatis were apparently randomly assaulting youths who they believed were involved in a local school boycott.

- On 1 January 1986 a large group of Mbokhoto vigilantes from Kwandebele abducted over 400 men and youths from the Moutse district (a district resisting the jurisdiction of the Kwandebele bantustan authorities) and were taken to a community hall in the capital of Kwandebele. There they were savagely beaten for several hours before being released. The Chief Minister of the bantustan supervised the assaults. Police have not as yet charged anyone.

- In Crossroads, vigilantes known as the Witdoeke did in a few days what government pressure, intrigue and repression had not been able to achieve in ten years: they demolished the well-known squatter camp and drove its residents out, rendering over 20,000 men, women and children homeless. Police are alleged to have co-ordinated the Witdoeke.

Examples of vigilante incidents cited by Nicholas Haysom, illustrating the effectiveness of the vigilantes as well as their relationship with the police, and how children and youths are affected.

A more recent, and a more sinister development, has been the incorporation of many of the vigilante elements within the formal state machinery, through the newly established kitskonstabels (Special Constables) and Municipal Police. The same elements will now operate armed legally.

More disturbing still has been the increasingly frequent assassination of anti-apartheid activists. It was at about the same time as the vigilante activity emerged that the assassination of anti-apartheid activists took on a broader significance.

To date none of the assassins of some 12 nationally known

anti-apartheid leaders has been identified, let alone brought to trial. This is in marked contrast to the rapid identification and prosecution of persons suspected of committing offences against the state. The actual assassination of activists is the tip of an iceberg of clandestine right-wing violence. In addition, numerous anti-apartheid activists have had their offices or their houses firebombed. For instance, large bombs destroyed the office block belonging to the Congress of South African Trade Unions (COSATU) in Johannesburg, and a second bomb only recently demolished an ensemble of offices housing anti-apartheid organisations including COSATU in Cape Town.

If the vigorous policing associated with the State of Emergency represents a short-term solution to South Africa's problems, the Joint Management Centres represent a longer-term and more sophisticated attempt to resolve the crisis. The Joint Management Centres are responsible only to the National Security Council, regarded as the most important decision-making body in the country. They are a network of 60 police and military security councils comprised of local security officials, business leaders, even government-designated black officials, who formulate local strategies and assist in incorporating local personalities into the security system. Chaired by a member of the security forces, these local cells have been criticised as not responsible to any constituency and as a way of deepening the militarisation of South Africa.

The committees structure aid and infrastructural development in a way which boosts government-supported black initiatives and strategies, including the re-introduction of community councillors. They co-ordinate a 'Hearts and Minds' programme, partly aimed at the youth and intended to inculcate acceptance of the government's policies and to undercut organisations leading resistance. Although the JMCs are supposedly advisory bodies, their operation works in tandem with the State of Emergency.

The pattern then is an ingenious one for the political and economic reconstruction of the townships. It appears to go as follows: community leaders are detained and vigilantes disrupt popular organisations; the organisational vacuum created by the detentions and intensified policing is filled by personalities and groups favourable to the government; when detainees are released or persons returned to the community, they are victimised by vigilantes or the police and rendered marginal. The Joint Management Centres then co-ordinate the injection of finance and infrastructural development in support of local bodies with a view to re-establishing the community council system and reconstructing the balance of forces in the townships. In some areas this strategy has proved effective.

This is really a large-scale and co-ordinated process of pacification no different from that pursued by an army of occupation and, like an army of occupation, the hardship it causes in human and material terms is considerable. The answer is not simply in a more humane police force – it lies in a police force accountable to the persons they police. More fundamentally it requires a government responsible to the people it governs.

A Lawyer's Experience

Peter Harris, a lawyer who has represented many detainees, and has represented trade unions and political activists.

In acting for the organisations that I represent I have been involved in a number of cases concerning children. These include applications to the Supreme Court for the release of child detainees and also applications to restrain the South African police from assaulting detainees, a number of whom have been children. In speaking of the South African police I refer also to the security forces of a number of the so-called homelands. By way of illustration let us look at the Bophuthatswana police.

The Bophuthatswana police in January and February of 1986 embarked on a systematic campaign of assault and terror in the Garankuwa area outside Pretoria. This campaign can only be described as brutal.

After over 120 affidavits and statements had been taken from ex-detainees, most of whom were children, the following pattern emerged. Bophuthatswana police units, armed with wire sjamboks, canes, batons, whips and rifles, conducted a series of mass arrests in Garankuwa which is a dormitory labour township for Pretoria. These raids occurred at schools and sports events, or children were even taken off the street. These child detainees, in groups of approximately 50, were arrested, locked into police trucks and taken to the Garankuwa police station. Behind the brick walls of the courtyard they were hit and kicked as they disembarked from the vehicles and were forced to run through a 'corridor' of armed policemen.

This corridor of assaults led to the white-tiled police mortuary. The children tell of the horror of the white tiles spattered, and in some places covered, with blood. Once, the mortuary doors were shut and they were instructed to strip naked and lie down face forwards on the floor.

Approximately 30 policemen would then enter the mortuary and at a given signal would proceed to thrash them with sjamboks and batons. In many cases these assault sessions lasted for hours as various policemen would tire and others would arrive to take their place.

These are not unsubstantiated allegations – almost every single affidavit that was taken was accompanied by a comprehensive medical report and photographs taken of the child detainees after their release.

The application for an interdict restraining all members of the Bophuthatswana police force at the Garankuwa police station from assaulting, unlawfully arresting, interfering with or victimising residents of Garankuwa was granted by consent. This means that the Bophuthatswana Government did not even oppose the granting of this interim interdict, so shocking and voluminous was the evidence against them. Today, almost two years after the assaults took place, those interim interdicts remain in force.

Now I tell you these things so that the reality of life in Bophuthatswana should be seen for what it is. It is important to realise also that the Bophuthatswana police who were responsible for this atrocity and the Winterveld massacre of April 1985 did not arise out of a vacuum. They were created, trained, armed and supplied by Pretoria, whose interests they protect.

Let me now return to the situation of the child detainee. To be a detainee in South Africa is to be removed from society, to be placed in a cell, sometimes alone and sometimes in large groups and small cells, and never to know when you will be released. The dangers to the mental and physical health of the detainee, particularly in the case of children, are enormous. Furthermore the anxiety engendered by removing detainees from their jobs and families affects mental and physical health as well.

In one particular case I represented a number of child detainees being held at the new Johannesburg prison. In affidavits placed before the Supreme Court the detainees alleged that warders at the prison had, over a number of days, been responsible for the indiscriminate assault and harassment of detainees, most of whom were children in that particular section of the prison.

In particular, they were forced to squat for lengthy periods of time, eat hot porridge with their bare hands and were placed in a confined area where they were viciously assaulted by a group of approximately 50 warders. Thereafter they were teargassed and placed back in their cells. As a result of those assaults certain of those detainees ended up in hospital. One whom I saw and whose mother brought this particular application, had a broken arm,

A young girl, 16 years of age, who lives in the township of Soweto, outside Port Elizabeth, was detained in a police raid. The raid consisted in the removal of the young people from their homes. They were then instructed to stand in rows facing a police truck. The lights of a vehicle were then switched on and it was clear to the child that the occupant of the vehicle was an informer and would point out those who were alleged to have done certain things.

The girl, later to be my client, was identified by the informer and told to step aside and get into a police truck. As she did so she was beaten with a sjambok several times. This method of detention is a common feature in the Eastern Cape. The girl was taken to the North End prison in Port Elizabeth and detained in terms of the Emergency Regulations. At the time of her detention her parents were not told why she was being arrested or where she was being taken. It was only one month later that they ascertained her whereabouts after many fruitless searches, and another two weeks before they were allowed to visit her.

However, as in the case of all other detainees, these visits were subject to various restrictions. She could only receive one visit per fortnight and then by only one parent at a time. Such visits are not contact visits but have to take place with a glass partition separating the detainee from the visitor. A prison warder sits next to the detainee throughout the visit and monitors the conversation. Detainees, including children, do not sleep on beds while in detention. Some sleep on a cold cement floor, protected only by a thin mat. For some there are no pillows or blankets. Often the food given to detainees including children is not fit for human consumption. Most detainees receive no fresh fruit or vegetables. Their diet consists mainly of bread, coffee and a strange looking liquid called soup. The bread is often mouldy. Many detainees, including children, have been hospitalised, suffering from malnutrition and depression caused by lack of vitamins. Imagine the effects of such a diet on the body of a growing child.

The Minister of Law and Order has stated that detainees are given the same food as that of an unmarried white policeman living in barracks. This is simply not true.

The attitude of the prison authorities towards child detainees is callous. I was told by my client that one night, unable to bear the thought of being detained any longer, she broke down and cried. Some of the other detainees followed suit. The prison warder's response to this, needless to say, was a total lack of concern. Their attitude was that the detainees were in need of male company and that is why they were upset.

The Minister of Law and Order gave the reasons for my client's detention as being the fact that she was a member of a street committee which the Minister regarded as an 'alternative structure' and therefore a threat to existing apartheid structures. According to the Minister then, she was a threat to public safety by virtue of her membership of a street committee and her detention was necessary to ensure the safety of the public.

A young girl's experience of detention. Cited by Vanessa Brereton, a Port Elizabeth lawyer active in political cases

---

severe bruises and concussion to the extent that he found it difficult to recall exactly what had happened. This case reveals systematic assaults, not isolated acts by rogue warders.

In many cases the police, when confronted in the legal arena, actually back down and release detainees. Although this retreat in many cases signals an acknowledgement that the original detention was unlawful, unnecessary or mala fide, it is my submission that the South African Minister of Law and Order often backs down to avoid the publicity that necessarily attaches itself to cases of this nature. An illustration of this was an application that I brought for the release of four detainees whose ages ranged from 12 years to 18 years. One of them was Moses Madia. [*His affidavit appears in Part 1*]

When notice was given to the police of this particular court application they immediately released the four child detainees and charged them with 'public violence' in the Protea Magistrates' Court in Soweto. After numerous court appearances over three months, the children came to court and were acquitted after it was found that the state had made out no case against them.

In another matter, that of Fanie Guduka, an 11-year-old child was charged with 'public violence'. He was refused bail by the magistrate on two occasions. He was eventually acquitted at the trial in which he was charged with public violence.

These are not isolated incidents. They fit into a general pattern of mass arrests, indefinite detention and only a few ensuing criminal trials that mostly result in the acquittal or withdrawal of charges against the children concerned.

The South African government is always quick to deny that detainees are tortured. It speaks easily of communist fabrications aimed only at discrediting the government. But the practice of electric shock treatment, for instance, is widely used in South Africa.

65

I want to relate to you an experience that I had recently of a mother. Her son was taken by the police on Monday morning. She was so shocked, so confused and so frightened when they came for her son that she had actually asked them if she could make herself a cup of coffee, could she please light a cigarette, could she give her son a warm jersey? She thought that by asking for these things, they would leave Mark alone, but only to notice that they would never leave Mark alone.

And after taking Mark away she said to herself – and while she was relating this to me, she was crying and shaking – she said that she never knew why she ever asked permission in her own home to make herself a cup of coffee. To give her own son a warm jersey.

Rashieda Abdulla, a full-time worker for the Call of Islam, established in 1984 to mobilise Muslims within the democratic movement

Some months ago a 16-year-old youth was referred to me by the Detainees' Parents Support Committee. He told me that he had been picked up the day before when he was walking in the street wearing a Free Mandela T-shirt. A panel van pulled up to the place where he was walking, some soldiers climbed out, and asked him for the address of a particular person. He replied that he didn't know where that person lived and he was pulled into the van.

When he was inside the van he realised that he was in a mobile torture chamber. Most of the seats had been taken out, there was a dynamo and battery on the floor of the van which then commenced to drive slowly through Diepkloof in Soweto. As they drove they applied electric shock treatment. Now electric shock torture is very difficult to prove since the signs and symptoms last for three days after the torture is given and in most cases detainees are kept in detention for lengthy periods of time.

When detainees are interrogated or tortured and in particular when given electric shock treatment they are normally released some months or weeks later, and one is never able to actually prove medically that they were in fact given electric shock torture. In this particular case, the authorities released him and he came into our offices the next day. We arranged for skin biopsies to be conducted on the hand that was given the electric shock treatment. When those tests were analysed by Professor Jonathan Gluckman, it was found that there were thermal burns on the hand consistent with electric shock torture.

To represent detainees legally in South Africa is a task that is made extremely difficult, both by the security legislation and a bureaucracy that is obstructionist. For example, the right of emergency detainees to legal counsel did not exist in South Africa. It was a right that had to be fought for and won in the Supreme Court (although a recent ruling has now rendered this right a privilege).

A minor gain, you might say, but detainees viewed that as a crucial gain as it effectively put an end to torture for those detainees that were fortunate enough to have legal representation and to be visited by lawyers. In essence lawyers were able to monitor the conditions and treatment of detainees they represented. However, the major problem which naturally remains is that there are too many detainees and there are too few lawyers.

In the early days of the 1986 State of Emergency there were approximately 10,000 detainees in jail. And if 800 or 1,000 of those were visited in the first one or two months of the emergency, I'd say it was a lot. A tragic situation.

From the start the authorities made it difficult to obtain access and information about detainees. To obtain information about detainees became a lengthy process involving telephone calls, telexes, letters, permits and negotiations, a process that in many cases can take up to two months.

It is not a coincidence that for the first three days of the 1986 State of Emergency, when thousands of people were being detained and their families were desperate for information, the telex machine of the South African Police in Pretoria mysteriously broke down resulting in an information blackout.

The point that must be made is that detainees in South Africa have very few rights and those few rights are under threat.

It would be wrong to suggest that only children bear the brunt of police action. The victims of the South African police are not only on the young but also the very old.

A person with whom I had contact in Fort Beaufort, a small rural town in the eastern Cape, was 75 years old at the time of her detention. When we inquired as to why she had been detained, the police gave the reason that she had been caught throwing stones. Now this may seem comical. It's not. She is a 75-year-old woman who nearly died in detention.

I've told you of only a few of the many abuses that are perpetrated upon children in South Africa. But can we ever comprehend the full sense of the hopelessness and the terror of a young child who suffers this type of humiliation and mutilation not only of the body but of the mind? It is indeed a sad day and a

great tragedy for our beloved country when a conference has to be
convened to discuss the torture and detention of its children.

Children in the Dock

*Johnny de Lange, a Cape Town lawyer who has been active in
defending youths charged with politically-related offences in
rural areas in the Western Cape*

The crime of public violence and some of the reactions of the
Supreme Court of the Western Cape provide some important
insights into the workings of the judiciary in these times of
upheaval in our country.

Firstly, a general observation: in this time of crisis, there can be
no doubt that the courts of our land have taken sides and that they
have on many occasions taken the side of the executive. This goes
beyond the more basic fact that our judiciary has to apply
apartheid laws and on numerous occasions has even extended the
powers of the executive and of the police.

I deal a lot with the crime of 'public violence' and most lawyers
who deal with human rights cases find that it is this crime that the
youth are most frequently charged with. Public violence is a
common law crime. It's not a crime created by parliamentary
statute and its Roman-Dutch heritage gives the charges a certain
legitimacy. It is important to note how the courts have reacted to
its very wide definition. Basically the offence is committed when
a number of people gather together, having a common purpose,
and the intention to disturb the public peace and tranquillity.

This definition itself is extremely wide, but our courts have
extended it even further. They have held that the word 'violence'
also implies a threat of violence. Therefore if I stand there with a
stick, or even if I'm just amongst a group of people who are
confronting the police, I could be found guilty of public violence.
So, on this one element the reach of the law has already been
extended tremendously.

As far as the element of common purpose is concerned, it can be
said that any gathering has a common purpose if it involves a
confrontation with the police, or any type of authority. So it is
clear that many acts of political dissent of this broad type would
usually fall within the ambit of this crime.

Sentencing in the case of this crime is another grave aspect. In
most crimes youth is regarded as a factor which is taken into
consideration for diminished responsibility or blameworthiness.
Our courts have held that in regard to this crime the 'interests of

society' take precedence. Apparently, society's interests are best served by sending juveniles to gaol. The usual sentence, in cases in the Western Cape, is imprisonment. This is even so when the people are juveniles, or if they are first offenders. At one stage, at the height of the unrest, a first offender and a juvenile could be given a sentence of between 4 to 7 years.

To show how the reach of this crime has been extended, I will use one case which came before Cape Supreme Court. There was a youth in Mitchells Plain who had a stone in his hand and there was general unrest in the area and he saw a police vehicle approaching. He lifted up his arm to throw the stone. He never got that far because his friends shouted that he mustn't do it. He threw down the stone. He ran away. The police chased him and caught him. He was found guilty of public violence although in fact he had not actually committed an act of violence.

Because this judgment was given by the Judge President of the Western Cape the reasoning permeated down the line to the magistrates who hear the cases in the first instance. These rulings have assisted the police in stamping out protest.

Another disturbing aspect of the administration of justice in the Western Cape is the fact that so-called political trials, especially involving appeals to the Supreme Court, are often heard by the same judges. Many believe that the effect is that the harsh rulings of the lower courts are frequently upheld.

A practical matter which is of increasing concern to lawyers is the unethical way in which some representatives of the state are acting in criminal matters. Usually lawyers have access to certain documents and certain types of information when defending a client. We are finding that prosecutors and state advocates now tend to keep those documents away from us and then spring them upon us at the most inopportune moments. Lawyers then experience great difficulty in getting an adjournment so as to look at the document.

Another thing, which has happened on two occasions and which has been upheld by the Supreme Court, is the hijacking of defence witnesses at court. The investigating officer approaches the witness at court and takes statements from him thus transforming them into state witnesses. One cannot then consult with them any more and cannot adequately prepare for the trial. Invariably what then happens is that the prosecutor does not use these witnesses.

These are practical instances of the extent to which the representatives of the state are prepared to go in these so-called 'politically coloured' trials.

69

In the rural areas intimidation by the legal system is rife. In one case about 23 school pupils were arrested and charged with public violence. These pupils were effectively denied legal defence. Lawyers present in the court had asked for further time to consult. This was refused. Discussions were then held with the Attorney-General of the Cape and his instructions were to oppose any application for postponement as this matter had to be completed as soon as possible. In the end most of the pupils were then convicted and sentenced to one year's imprisonment. The matter was then taken on review. In discussions with the office of the Attorney-General their simple explanation was that in the rural areas people have to be taught a lesson: that we have got to finish the case as quickly as possible so that the people in those rural areas will learn a lesson and not persist in their activities. Now this reminds one of the early sixties when the state thought they could crush the movement with their harsh sentences.

Ramesh Vassen, a lawyer from the Western Cape

For these reasons it should be clear that the solution doesn't really lie in the law per se, and it lies with the grassroots. Our lawyers should start playing a more active role in working for a just society. We should start exposing both atrocities and the abuse of the criminal justice system.

CHILDREN IN DETENTION

One evening at the conference Beyers Naude read from a press statement issued by South Africa's Law and Order Minister Adriaan Vlok singling out the Detainees' Parents Support Committee as the source of 'false and slanted allegations and information . . . committed in (sic) propagating biased and untested information . . . wild claims of mass detentions of children and their so-called torture and abuse'. This attack on the credibility of the DPSC with its veiled threat of a possible banning was just another round in the state's attempt to silence the effective network of monitoring organisations which the DPSC has built countrywide. Mr Vlok's statement cast a brief shadow of fear – no delegate coming from inside South Africa could be immune from arrest, interrogation, detention or torture if the Minister should order that action on his or her return. But a stronger sentiment was scepticism towards the Minister's 'appeal . . . to bring such evidence [of torture and abuse] to the South African police for thorough investigation'. So well known is the DPSC for the conservative nature of its estimates that the 8,800 children it announced had been detained in the preceding two years is indelibly marked in South African minds. Minister Vlok's assertion that no child under 15 was in detention during the Harare Conference was widely disbelieved. His figure of 115 children currently in detention, in line with the DPSC's own figures, did nothing to undermine the confidence in the DPSC's overall estimates. 'Though 115 is 115 too many', as Beyers Naude put it.

Overview

Detainees' Parents Support Committee

Apartheid has spawned a system of child detention. The Detainees' Parents Support Committee (DPSC) was formed in 1981 to help parents whose children were detained.

Our estimates are conservative. When the Minister reveals lists of detainees, we invariably find names of people whom we did not know about. We make every attempt to confirm the names and numbers of people in detention by speaking to lawyers, community organisations and welfare organisations. The Children's Act in South Africa defines a child as a person below the age of 18 years.

71

I was taken from my home at about 1 am by the SAP and Administration Board Officers and then to the police station. From the police station I was taken to the prison where I was held until I was released two months later.

There were seven of us. Four girls and three boys. The boys were put in one cell and the girls in another. I was interrogated three times for about seven hours at a time. During the interrogations I was made to stand all the time and was beaten by my interrogators who were all policemen. There were four black policemen who interrogated me. During the interrogations I was given no food or drink and was refused permission to go to the toilet.

A 16-year-old girl's experience, cited by the DPSC

When releasing statistics of children held, the Minister of Law and Order defines children as under the age of 16 years. This has the effect of making official figures falsely low for child detainees.

In 1982, one year after the DPSC was started, 8 people under the age of 18 were detained under security legislation. During the 1986 State of Emergency of the 22,000 detainees, 8,800 were children under 18 (most of them between the ages of 13 and 18). Some of them were under the age of 9. As at 22.9.87 the numbers of children detained under the June 1987 State of Emergency (according to records entered thus far) were 180. Of these 112 are still in detention. By 22.9.87 one of these children had spent 485 days in detention.

Statements from former child detainees suggest that a reason for the detentions is an attempt to recruit informers. Methods ranging from death threats to monetary reward are used by the security police to exert pressure on young people. Assault and torture are used on these children in order to extract information as well as to strike fear into their hearts.

Children are detained from a variety of places. They are often at home asleep in their beds when the police arrive. They may be at school or simply walking or playing in the streets. Recently in Parliament, Helen Suzman told of a new practice in the Eastern Cape: vehicles with darkened windows travel through the streets. The police sit in these vehicles with informers who point out people in the street. Anyone who is pointed out is immediately detained.

Children may be caught up in the process of detention even when they are not the specific objects of detentions. An example of a Soweto family comes to mind. Early one morning the police arrived to detain an 18-year-old son. On being told that he was not home, they promptly arrested the entire family including a one-month baby and four other children aged 5, 6, 10 and 15 years. There are other cases of such 'hostage taking'.

A common pattern of detention has emerged from information collected by the DPSC. A child is arrested and taken to a police station. There, he or she is assaulted and questioned for a few hours and then taken to a cell in the police station or a prison. They may spend weeks or months in the cell before being interrogated again or released.

It is illegal to publicise the circumstances of, or treatment in, detention of a person detained under Regulation 3 of the Emergency Regulations. The penalty for infringing this regulation is a fine of up to R20,000 or imprisonment for up to 10 years. The evidence of detention conditions available to the South African public comes mainly from court cases. A court application in Grahamstown in 1985 revealed that the food available to detainees in one detention centre was so inadequate as to amount to a 'starvation diet'.

The suffering of children in detention begins even before birth. The DPSC has documented a number of cases of pregnant women who are detained with limited access to medical care. For instance, a woman held in Kimberley under Emergency detention is seven months pregnant. She was detained in April 1987 and managed to see her lawyer five months later. She has not visited an ante-natal clinic, nor is she on a supplemented diet. She has not received iron or vitamin tablets. There have also been reports of pregnant women who have had miscarriages in detention. In an East London prison, a detainee alleged that she had to deliver another detainee's baby at night because no other assistance was available.

The previous State of Emergency regulations allowed for one hour's exercise, the present State of Emergency allows for half an hour per day. One of the reasons for the shorter exercise time is the overcrowding of the prisons.

We have received complaints from released detainees regarding inadequate medical attention, such as the following examples: a district surgeon examining people in groups of eight or more; people being told to stand in rows with their shirts off; prescriptions without proper examination.

Child detainees are not treated differently from adult detainees. In fact, children have been held in the same cells as adult common criminals. There have been reports of child abuse and rape.

In the previous emergency, most of the children were held in

At first we were about seven in the cell. The food we were given was not enough. We had to share from one plate. We were given porridge and tea for breakfast, porridge and soup for lunch and porridge and coffee for the evening meal. We slept on mats on the floor. Three people had to share one mat and we were each given one blanket. We were very cold. I did not see my parents at all during the first two months. We were not given any change of clothing and had to make do with the clothes we were wearing when we were detained. We had to wash them ourselves. We had no hot water and had to shower in cold water. We had no books, magazines or games at all.

I was arrested with 23 other people and after the first two months we were all taken to another prison. When we were moved, more children were brought in and eventually we were about 37 in the cell.

A 13-year-old boy whose three months in detention were described to the DPSC

overcrowded cells. It appears that up to 40 people were held together in one cell. Many children reported that they were not allowed to exercise (despite the regulations).

There have been reports pre-dating the 1985 emergency of children being raped while in detention. During 1985-6 there was an acute shortage of food at Diepkloof Prison. A newspaper carried a story of young people selling their bodies to common criminals in exchange for food.

Although the regulations applying in this State of Emergency appear to allow for improved conditions of detention, we see little cause for optimism. Children in detention are at the mercy of the prison authorities, who are indemnified by the State of Emergency. It is still illegal to publicise conditions within the prisons. The Minister is not obliged to furnish reasons for detention and detainees do not have right of access to legal counsel. In short, despite the fact that detainees have awaiting-trial-prisoner status on paper, there is no way of guaranteeing their rights. This is particularly alarming for those who are now well into the second year of their detention. The spectre of indefinite incarceration looms over them.

Torture and Assault in Detention

During the State of Emergency, the courts have granted urgent interdicts restraining the police from assaulting detainees.

Recently, the Commissioner of Police ordered investigations

into allegations of torture by two children, aged 15 and 17 years. The 17-year-old boy (Reuben) claimed that he had been beaten with quirts 80–86 times. Thereafter, 5 litres of petrol were allegedly poured over him and a white policeman allegedly urinated in his face. He claimed that the police threatened to set him alight and took him to a field and placed a tyre around his neck.

Reuben was examined by two doctors after his release. Both doctors found he had more than 40 lashes on his back. A criminal charge brought by the state against two policemen and one soldier ended in acquittal in August 1987. The court found that there was 'conflicting evidence'. A signed doctor's certificate attesting sjambok wounds on Reuben's back is evidence enough for us.

Children are usually required to answer questions or make statements regarding events and other people. Many children report being hit with fists, quirts (or sjamboks), and rifle butts or having been kicked. Attempts to throttle the child are common. This may occur while the child is hooded so that his torturers cannot be identified, and also to increase feelings of disorientation. There appears to be little discrimination as to whether the child is hit or kicked. The most common areas of assault are the back, buttocks, legs, head and face and hands. Some children report being beaten under their feet until their feet are bruised.

Apartheid's ugliness is most vividly expressed in the rural areas and the so-called 'homelands'. Yet their remoteness denies them publicity and its concomitant support. The isolation of the rural areas means that people have very limited access to lawyers or even to knowledge of their rights under the Emergency Regulations.

Even more worrying is the limited access that these detainees have to medical care. Many of the prisons close to the cities do not have full-time doctors in attendance. In the rural areas, one district surgeon will cover three or more prisons in different towns.

While DPSCs exist in rural communities, they face severe repression and their members are often detained and their offices raided. For example, in April of this year, one of our advice offices in Pietersburg was raided. Two of the field workers were detained and all documents confiscated. They are still in detention.

Children on trial

The incarceration of children for political offences is not confined to Emergency detention. Over the last two years, tens of thousands of people have been arrested and charged with public violence.

Since the declaration of the State of Emergency on 12 June 1986 the Detainees Support Committee has been experiencing immense problems coping with detentions in Natal. Almost every community, every town and village was affected directly or indirectly.

It was difficult monitoring detentions. People have been picked up off the streets, taken from their homes in the early hours of the morning, and arbitrarily detained by the military in door-to-door searches. Our estimates of the number of detentions are conservative. For example, there is a community just north of Pietermaritzburg called Greytown and there on one afternoon the police and military moved in and arbitrarily detained people. They picked up about 200 people.

These people were taken to the local police station and broken up into two groups of 100 each. Because the police station was not large enough to accommodate all of them, 100 of them were released and the other 100 were detained. We only received information about the people who were being held there a month later. Most of them had been assaulted whilst they were in detention.

In Natal as in other provinces, it is the youth who continue to bear the brunt of security force action. In fact more than half of the total number of people detained in Natal are youths under the age of 19.

During the two weeks preceding the first anniversary of the State of Emergency, prison doors in Natal opened briefly and then slammed shut again. Quite a number of people were released but the euphoria was short lived. Over 90 per cent of those released were forced into hiding, too afraid to go home for fear of right-wing Inkatha vigilante attacks.

One 17-year-old said: 'All that has happened is that we have been released from a small prison into a much larger one. We have been released into our townships where we have become prisoners in our own homes.' Another detainee commented: 'We have been released into the hands of right-wing vigilantes and security forces. We know they have orders to shoot. We will remain detainees until we have won our freedom.'

In the period following the re-imposition of the emergency, that is from 12 June 1987, we have witnessed a new trend in detentions, outside both emergency detentions and the Internal Security Act. People are basically detained for very short periods, ranging from two or three hours to two or three days. In that period they are quite vigorously interrogated and almost always assaulted.

This is borne out by the experience of a 15-year-old youth from Chesterville township which is just outside Durban. He said that he was at home and at midnight someone kicked the door down and came in wearing a balaclava. They dragged him out of the house and into a military vehicle. He could not recognise the people who did it because they were wearing balaclavas and he was taken to the local police station where a hood was pulled over his head. He was then taken into the bush where he was questioned and tortured for about three or four hours. After which he was once again put into the truck and taken to another section of the township and released.

There is one other example of courage and commitment that I would like to share. It was about a week after the State of Emergency was declared last year and there were quite a number of detentions in northern Natal. A youth came to the DPSC office again. It was obvious that he was fatigued, very tired. He hardly had clothes on him and it was winter. His shoes were completely worn out. I asked him what was wrong and he said that he was tired. I asked him where he was from and he said he was from a place about 250-300 kilometres away from Durban. And I asked him then, why have you come here, and he said – I have got a list of names of my comrades who have been detained, please help.

I asked him how he came and he told me, he ran. He ran for three days between 250-300 kilometres to our offices with that information, asking for help. And that wasn't the end of it. We did whatever we could and then we tried to give him some money to go back and buy himself shoes at least, because his shoes were worn our. He took the money and said he was not going to use it to buy shoes. 'This money,' he said, 'I am going to use for my comrades up there. We can't live at home and we are going to use it to buy food.' I thought I knew about commitment, but when I saw this youth, I couldn't say anything. I was just shocked.

Examples cited by Hans Ramrak, a DPSC worker in Natal

These cases take up to six months to appear in court and the accused often spend this time in prison either because they are refused bail or because they appear in court undefended and are not aware that they have the right to apply for bail.

Although the DPSC has no reliable statistics available on the number of children charged with public violence, it is reasonable to assume that the percentage is similar to the percentage of detainees under 18 years of age.

In the DPSC office, we have seen several cases of children, who

There was a young girl who was in detention with me. She was detained before me and she stayed on after me. I think she spent ten months in detention. This girl was a young schoolgirl. She used to stay with us, five in the cell. She was a schoolgirl who wants to study, who wants to be a future leader of South Africa, who wants to be something for her nation. But because of the government she didn't write exams in 1985. In 1986 she was supposed to write exams but she was detained.

She wanted to study while she was inside. She would take her books and sit down and look at them, but then she would say to us: 'Now, I can't think, my mind is blank. I can't concentrate, I don't know how I am going to go on.' I used to try and explain to her, please come down and study a little bit, if you can. And we used to be quiet for half an hour for her to study, but she began to cry in the middle of her studying, telling us that she doesn't know how she feels, she doesn't know what to do, she doesn't want to be here, she wants to get out and study, because the other children are going to write exams and she is not going to write.

We used to comfort her, but in the middle of the night she used to get up and sit on the bottom of your bed and wake you up and ask, 'What must I do because I feel like breaking down?' I used to say to her, 'Please don't break down because the enemy is going to enjoy it. You must be brave and strong.' And she asked me – 'be brave and do what?' I said – 'There is nothing you can do inside, you must sit and wait till the government will release you.'

But because the government wants to torture us as parents, they just put us there and then leave us there. The thing that is so bad, is to sit with a young child in detention. I never tried to think about myself, I always thought about the other children in hiding outside. I never used to think about my children. I know my son was in hiding too, but I used to think about the children of Africa, who want to achieve something, who want to be leaders of tomorrow, who want to see something done, to abolish this apartheid regime.

Dorothy Mfako, a leading member of the United Women's Congress in the Western Cape

were held for many months, thereafter being charged with public violence. It appears that the state uses such charges to justify the initial detention, particularly as charges are withdrawn in the majority of cases. Too few of them have come to court to allow us to make a meaningful statistical analysis.

In many cases children are being brought to court without legal representation. Other cases are known in which the child is charged and sentenced without his/her parents being informed of their child's court appearance. Even in those cases where the children have attorneys, children are sometimes brought to court without the attorney having been informed. We must also surely question the integrity of a court that will accept as evidence, statements made by children who have spent months in prison. Children held incommunicado, at the mercy of the authorities, are highly vulnerable to coercion.

Many released children become internal refugees. They fear that, if they return home after they have been released, they will be harassed and their families endangered. An 18-year-old matric pupil has been told that he should never have been released and the police were conducting a search for him. They badgered his father as to his son's whereabouts. The police also visited his school. This young man has had to leave his township and has become a refugee within his own country.

There are a growing number of such cases. These people lose contact with social support structures. They are isolated and often desperate. Some are pressured into working for the government or joining vigilante groups. In this way we see the victims of repression being forced to assist their own oppressors. In other cases they are harassed by vigilantes. Possibly even more alarming, and reflective of the cynicism of the state, is the assassination of young people, with increasing frequency.

The South African government realises that without international news coverage of events in South Africa, international pressure on them will wane. Our aim is to break this 'blanket of silence'.

Teaching under the State of Emergency

A teacher in the Western Cape

During the emergency of 1985 I was in detention and shared a block of cells with five schoolchildren from Worcester, ranging from 14 to 16 years of age.

There were 15 of us in a cell and I think all the older detainees there felt obliged to give some support to those schoolchildren. Some of us were forced to stay in isolation for about five days before being moved to a communal cell. At first we found that some of the youths were very strong in the cell there. The youngest one, 14 years of age, was interrogated by the Security

The testimony which I wish to give relates to my own experiences and observations during the State of Emergency. Children all over the Western Cape were teargassed or beaten up. Nursery school children witnessed these actions, or woke up in the morning to find that a parent, or a brother, or a sister had been detained during the night, or had simply disappeared.

My own child was 3 years old when her father was detained during the early hours of the morning. When she asked for her daddy the next morning I did not yet know how to explain what had happened. I fabricated a story that her daddy had gone to the mountain to fetch her a monkey. A few weeks later she asked me whether the monkey was in jail. Soon she refused to attend creche unless her daddy would fetch her. During that time she often slept restlessly and fell off the bed almost every night.

I eventually took her to see her father when he indicated that he could not remember her face. I asked her to be brave, not to cry. She didn't, although the tears streamed down her father's face. However when she came outside she wept very bitterly and other mothers reprimanded me for bringing her along. She said through her tears, 'The mountain is not inside'.

The effect of that experience on my daughter, who is now 5, is her understanding of the police. Today she vividly recalls how the police teargassed people coming out of church after a candle-light vigil, even though she was asleep in my arms at the time.

One day recently, we drove past the police station when suddenly she raised her fist in the air and shouted 'Amandla!' In general South African black children are robbed of their childhood. Unlike children elsewhere they do not play creative games, instead they have joined in the struggle for liberation.

A social psychologist in the Western Cape

Police and asked to give names and to spy on what the other comrades were saying and doing in the cells. He refused and the SP forced him to spend more days in isolation. As time went on, the detention had its effect on the children. There were nights when these youths would sob bitterly, some would go into deep depression. We the older comrades there would try our best to pacify them but it wasn't an easy task. We took turns to give some support to them but later it had an effect on us as well, because we felt equally depressed.

They remained in detention the longest. As the older comrades were released, these youths were left behind. It was heart-breaking to leave them behind.

There were young persons in detention in other parts of the jail. We did not see them but we often heard their cries and we made some representations to the prison authorities to get some assistance for them. But it didn't help much. But on one occasion, a young person was admitted who we thought was mentally disabled. He had no idea of where he came from, why he was there or what he had done. And we did make representations to the prison authorities and he was released after about five days in detention.

We were aware that the authorities were denying the existence of child detainees. We vowed that we would try and highlight the position of these five schoolchildren. Some of us placed an advert in the local papers on our release, making known the detention of these children. We mentioned their names in the advert as well. The Minister of Police at the time actually denied that there were such children in prison and this frustrated us very much, and made us feel extremely helpless.

Another incident I want to describe was the mass arrest in 1985 of an entire school. This school had about 800 pupils. After minor incidents which could have been handled by the school authorities, the police arrived in convoys of trucks.

All 800 children present in the school, ranging in ages from 12 to 19, were instructed to remain in their rooms and armed policemen patrolled the corridors to prevent anybody from leaving. Thereafter every child was loaded on to the trucks and taken to the local police station, and held for some five hours while they were interrogated. The whole exercise was a terrifying experience for the children.

While they were being loaded on to the trucks they were filled with fear, especially the younger ones. One must remember that in South Africa, the police force has a very negative image and young children learn this early in their life. They learn this on the streets of the townships because the smallest crime in the area is treated with brute force.

As teachers at that particular school we found ourselves in a dilemma because in a normal school situation, as teachers, we are supposed to give guidance, advice and support to our schoolchildren at all times. We did not know what to say to them. There were many questions from these young persons. What would happen to them at the police cell, could they be beaten, could they be held for a long time? These were questions posed to us. Some of us tried our best to calm them. Some of the schoolchildren virtually fainted. Some of them had nervous breakdowns. And the

While I was in detention our little boy of 4 years old found it very difficult to understand why I was not able to call home and at least talk to him. And since I wasn't calling them he asked his mother: 'Can I call my daddy, where is he?' And he found it very difficult to work this through. And after I came out of detention, every single morning for quite a time the first thing that he would do when he woke up was to get up and ask if I was there. Indelibly impressed upon his mind are the two police stations where I was kept before I was taken to prison. It's impressed on his mind and he will carry it for the rest of his life with him.

I want to highlight one piece of legislation dealing with children. The Child Care Act is the mechanism by which society can give protection to children who are not taken care of adequately. Provision is made in the legislation for adoption and foster care, etc. The primary focus is to actually intervene in situations where children are not being taken care of adequately.

What is required to effect such action, to deal with the needs of children? There must be a report by a social worker. The purpose of the report is to do a psycho-social investigation to assess the circumstances and then to make recommendations. The social worker has to come before a magistrate in a children's court enquiry and make recommendations upon which a final assessment is made.

The present situation in the country has totally overtaken the provisions of this legislation. We are in a situation where those who should be the protectors of children have become the chief perpetrators of atrocities against them. It has been my duty, on many occasions, to go and preach unity at funerals where children have been killed, murdered by security forces. The youngest was a 3-year-old child who was killed and the police, after having shot the child, said to the parents, 'Don't be concerned, it was just rubber bullets that we used.' Three pathologists were needed to make an assessment and only the third one was able to say that the ammunition was the kind used on the border between Namibia and Angola.

Since we recognise that the state does not protect children but is the chief perpetrator of atrocities, what we social workers need to do in the community is to engage in protection of our children to the best of our ability in order to get them through this period. And we have seen some evidence of this as more and more parents have begun to develop an understanding of what their children are all about in terms of the struggle that is being waged.

The second piece of action is the need for mass mobilisation because it's very evident that unless we eradicate apartheid from our society there will never be protection for our children and already it is 11 years since Soweto '76. How much longer do we have to stay in this kind of situation? We again appeal to the international community to stand firmly with us. Thank you.

Reverend Lionel Louw of the African Methodist Episcopal Church and Chairperson of the Western Province Council of Churches – he is a social worker

---

police actually refused us permission to give them support or medication.

We carried out some schoolchildren from the classrooms, and then we were followed by a policeman. I would not say that many schools of children have been detained in the same way, but certainly the police presence in our schools has become very common and there are very many examples of this.

I think sometimes not enough focus is given to the kind of police repression directed at the schools. Often between the time we arrive at school and the time we leave, there is some police presence.

When there were some incidents at our schools and the police moved in and teargassed the schoolchildren, many of them would flee and dive over the fences. During 1985, as well, huge fences about 6 feet high with pointed ends were placed around all our schools. And we felt that one of the reasons that they put up these high fences was to prevent the children from escaping.

Then also they placed security guards at our school gates so we had to check in and out, and the children were strictly controlled. In a sense then, as far as we were concerned, many of our schools had become detention camps during school hours.

CHALLENGE TO THE INTERNATIONAL MEDICAL COMMUNITY

In mid-1985 a young South African district surgeon, Dr Wendy Orr, briefly made headlines around the world with her exposure of police brutality against detainees in prison in Port Elizabeth. Her evidence came from her routine duties of examining detainees. In an unprecedented case by a government doctor she made a court application with 42 other people for an injunction restraining the police from assaulting detainees in the area. A temporary injunction was granted by the court and a year later the Minister of Law and Order agreed to pay the legal costs of her case. But this hard-won legal and moral victory, far from opening a new chapter in the acceptable treatment of detainees, was simply covered over as the tide of emergency detentions ebbed and flowed. Dr Wendy Orr was ostracised by her colleagues and squeezed out of the prison service.

Her own statement and those of other contributors in this section make a scathing indictment of the record of South Africa's professional bodies in the medical sphere. In contrast, doctors like those who participated in the Harare Conference have, through their work with the DPSC and in their care for released detainees, provided a monitoring network whose evidence of the extent of torture nation-wide is irrefutable. Dr Wendy Orr's personal experience in the jails of Port Elizabeth and her extrapolation of 'thousands and thousands' of such assaults all over South Africa is borne out by the experiences of others. All these health professionals called on their colleagues of the international community to break 'the deafening silence' around the abuse of their profession in South Africa.

Caring for Detainees

Dr Greg McCarthy, a lecturer in medicine at the University of Witwatersrand, and a member of the DPSC and of NAMDA (The National Medical and Dental Association)

Doctors in South Africa who make public statements regarding their patients are sometimes accused of breaching confidentiality and thereby acting unethically. I believe it is the ethical duty of all doctors in South Africa to speak out now against the brutality that is being meted out to our children and our people. At last we are beginning to talk about Nuremberg principles. Do medical

84

professionals in South Africa expect to be overlooked when that time comes?

The National Medical and Dental Association is a non-racial organisation of doctors and dentists which is committed to providing equal and accessible health care to the people of South Africa. We run a medical service for released detainees.

In May, June and July of 1987 the service saw 83 children. That means one child a day. Of these 13 were female and 70 were male. Sixty-eight of the children were aged between 15 and 17 years. Now three-quarters of these children, 73 per cent had been in detention for in excess of 20 weeks. Sixty-four of them complained of assault, but bearing in mind that they had been in detention for more than 20 weeks and that assault usually occurs early on in that detention process, it is not surprising that only 4 per cent showed scars. The psychological scars were much more evident and equally important. In fact 57 per cent, more than half, of those children had psychological symptoms, and one third, 32 per cent – one in three children – had a definable psychiatric illness.

Fourteen of these children had been subjected to electric shocks, they said, and 13 to solitary confinement. Now these figures refer to children who have access both to the DPSC office in Johannesburg and to an urban-based clinic. We have no reason to believe that the situation is better in the rural communities, and every reason to believe that it is worse.

Recently conditions of treatment of political detainees were highlighted at a law students' conference. An official of the Transkei's Social Welfare Programme alleged that almost every person who had been detained had been tortured or suffered general ill-treatment at the hands of the authorities. In one case a 17-year-old boy was subjected to the so-called TV treatment. This involves placing a canvas bag full of water over the detainee's head thereby suffocating him or her. This 17-year-old allegedly coughed blood and his eyes were damaged at the end of this terrible 'game'. The detainee was held in solitary confinement and later charged with arson. At the trial no enquiries were made as to whether he would be represented by a legal adviser despite the court's knowledge that the 17-year-old had no knowledge of court procedure and despite the fact that they were aware that he had been held incommunicado in solitary confinement.

Here is one story which will give you an idea of conditions in our country from a parent's perspective. Mrs M is a mother of five, in her forties. Her youngest child is three years old. One of her teenagers was detained last year. Mrs M herself has recently spent

85

more than a year in prison, was charged and recently released on bail, but not allowed to go home. She is suffering acutely from the psychological effects of prolonged solitary confinement.

Imagine this woman's anguish when after being released, she is put into a different kind of prison. She is kept in a hostel, away from her loved ones and her family, where she is alone because she is the only woman there. She is in a room on her own. Having spent a year in solitary confinement, she comes out to conditions like that. It is difficult as a therapist of any kind to be able to respond to that woman's anguish and psychological pain.

The only light on the horizon for Mrs M was the fact that her 3-year-old child had been sneaked to her in the hostel where she was living, and by the time I saw her she was already starting to improve. But she was intensely fearful that her son would be removed from her and was there anything that I could do about that? As a doctor, my prescription for her, instead of being pills or anti-depressants, was to write a note prescribing that her son be allowed to stay with her. I had to prescribe that a mother and son should be together. A society in which doctors have to do that is the real patient here. We have to redouble our efforts to end apartheid society. It is a matter of preventative medicine.

The Psychology of Torture

Don Foster, Professor in Psychology at the University of Cape Town and author of Detention and Torture in South Africa *with Dennis Davis and Diane Sadler (published by James Currey, London, 1988)*

It is my contention that torture is a fundamental part of the fundamental system of apartheid. It is central to the maintenance of power and, as such, torture is quite clearly a political act. Torture is part of the legal system in South Africa, made possible by laws which allow detention without trial.

What is torture? I'm not sure that one can ever adequately define torture. Nevertheless let me highlight some of the aspects which may be useful in thinking about it. According to the United Nations, the following characteristics are important elements of torture: it is an intentional act, not an accident; secondly, it is an act performed by public officials acting in their public capacity; thirdly, it is the infliction of pain and suffering; fourthly, and very importantly, the definition regards the infliction of psychological pain or stress as torture.

The pain, the suffering, the destruction of human beings with the more sophisticated use of psychological torture is as inhumane as any affliction of physical pain, yet it leaves no tell-tale marks.

The United Nations goes on to say that no state may ever condone torture. War, internal conflict, and States of Emergency can never provide a justification for torture.

The psychological modes of torture are less well known than the physical. There are four different groups of psychological torture.

The first are communication techniques such as false accusations, misleading information (such as false reports of the accidental death of a relative). The second form includes mental weakening devices, solitary confinement, prolonged interrogation, prolonged confinements, blindfolding, hooding, and sleep deprivation. The idea is to weaken a person so fundamentally that they break down and provide the information which the security police want.

The third form may be regarded as psychological terror tactics such as threats of violence to their family or to their friends or witnessing the torture of others. Youngsters have reported hearing screams from neighbouring cells. That is as frightening as being hammered oneself. A technique in South Africa has been sham executions, for example, putting a gun to a prisoner's head, and more recently putting a tube around the neck of the detainee and threatening to set it alight. Finally, the fourth form of psychological torture is humiliation. Nakedness and verbal abuse aims to degrade the fundamental humanity of the person.

What about the effects, the aftermath of torture?

Firstly, I want to raise some conceptual issues in thinking about the aftermath of torture. The effects of torture start before torture has started, although that may sound paradoxical. Our own research indicated that 60 per cent of Section 29 detainees that we interviewed had been harassed before their detention. In our view prior harassment heightens the fear of a detainee. He feels as if he is under the particular scrutiny of the state, singled out as a target, and is fully aware of what happens to detainees. A sense of dread accompanies him into detention.

If the effects of detention start before detention, they continue inside detention. The psychological effects inside detention weaken people and reduce them to a state of psychological dependence and helplessness. The system of detention and torture in South Africa is a closed system, a system of total isolation, with the individual placed entirely in the hands of the security police and state officials. The detainee is entirely

87

Sipho – as I shall call him – was a 22-year-old law student. He walked into my office one day and said, 'I had to write an exam this morning. I sat in the room for 20 minutes and then walked out. I came straight here. There's something wrong with me, I think I'm going mad.'

Just before the exam he had told the lecturer 'I am tired. I cannot write'. The lecturer, an Afrikaner, interpreted his words literally and told him 'It is an official examination and you must write.'

Sipho comes from a rural community about 400 kilometres outside of Cape Town. He was the only child of his family who reached university, as are many of our black students. His family was financially responsible for his studies. He then, in respect of his family, had quite some guilt that already they are so impoverished and he was having to take from them and now not writing an examination.

Sipho has not been able to see them since his release from his latest detention in September. He had some concerns about his home community. He had been very active in that particular community. Leadership at that time was in hiding and he was concerned that organisations were splitting, organisations were in distress. He was both an informal and formal leader to people there. So he felt guilt and impotence in respect of his rural community, as if he had let them down.

Sipho had had numerous detentions as a student. He was also detained for a month in 1985 in terms of the Emergency Regulations. His last detention was from June to September in 1986. When he spoke to me it was the first time that he ever spoke to anybody about the detention experience. He claimed to have been in solitary confinement, to have been tortured, humiliated, interrogated with sleep deprivation.

After his detention Sipho experienced himself in a very different way. That is why he thought that he was going mad. He was depressed, he couldn't concentrate, he was distracted. He said to me 'Sometimes I lie in my room for hours and I have to think "What am I thinking?"' The things that he was interested in previously he had lost all interest in. He did not want to talk with people. He found himself at numerous times almost inappropriately reliving the experience. The detention experience would recur in a very intrusive manner. He also had survivor guilt, feeling guilty for having left comrades behind in the cell, also feeling guilty about the fact that he was scared at times while he was there or that he cried while he was there. He also experienced physical symptoms such as inability to fall asleep or when he does sleep having the most awful nightmares. He had loss of energy, loss of appetite. He had pervasive headaches since September. He was treated by a doctor symptomatically, the headaches never disappeared, the doctor kept giving tablets. He experienced social isolation withdrawing from the local community where he boarded and the campus community. It was as if he had created a barrier between himself and others who might have been reaching out for him. Whereas before he was involved in the campus organisations, he no longer did so.

This exam that Sipho did not write was a final examination. If he didn't write that exam he would have to repeat his second year. The disorientation, the psychic scarring that Sipho experiences could be the testimony of every detainee.

A student counsellor

---

dependent on their captors, even to the fundamentals of life as well as their eventual release. Lack of adequate responsibility for oneself in that situation in combination with other factors can lead to chronic depression.

The official figures of those who have died in the South African detention system are over 60, and if you add in those who have died in custody in politically-coloured circumstances, that figure rises to about 90.

The effects of detention there are potentially devastating and long lasting. They include fatigue and physical disability, weight loss, appetite loss, sleep disorders, cognitive impairment, memory problems, concentration problems, behavioural changes, psychosomatic problems, trembling, diarrhoea, stomach problems, stomach aches, depression, anxiety. Anxiety, a common feature, runs right through these things.

In our own research we discovered extensive damage to interpersonal relationships. People come out of detention, and instead of being in warm good interpersonal relationships, families break up. The destructive interpersonal effects are overwhelming. Instead of being able to go back to supportive comrades people are irritable, jumpy and suspicious. This loss of trust in human nature is perhaps the most tragic of all the effects. There are also effects on families, on friends, on comrades. Often there is a splitting of these units and a heightened vulnerability on release.

If torture has these effects on individuals, if it has these effects on families and friendship systems, it also has effects on political organisations themselves. These effects are contradictory. There is no doubt that the aim of detention and torture is to destroy political organisations. There is no doubt that it can weaken resistance. However, in the long run the notion that people can be governed by intimidation and repression is false. These and other acts of inhumanity tend to create commitment and breed resistance.

I believe that we should fight for the legal recognition that psychological factors constitute a part of torture and in particular that evidence and information extracted through psychological duress should be inadmissible.

We must also recognise the degree to which the South African state depends on torture. That recognition alone is important. The actions of professional bodies in South Africa by and large in this terrain have been abysmal. It is part of the role of the international community to put substantial pressure on those professional bodies.

Finally, I want to make it quite clear that I recognise that the only solution to combat torture in South Africa, is, in Frank Chikane's words, to fight for the ultimate removal of the apartheid system.

Call to the International Community

Dr Wendy Orr, formerly a state-employed district surgeon whose work involved visiting detainees

In July 1985, when the first State of Emergency was declared, I was employed by the Department of Health as the district surgeon in Port Elizabeth. I was one of the privileged few who was legally obliged and permitted to see detainees. From the first day that I started to see State of Emergency detainees I was overwhelmed by an endless stream of literally hundreds of beaten, wounded and distressed people. Not all were children, obviously, but a number were below 18 years of age and the majority were young adults in their early twenties.

Many of the cases illustrated a variety of torture methods; firstly, the agonising anticipation of waiting to be called to Security Branch headquarters and every day, seeing comrades come back beaten and degraded; secondly, the use of threats; thirdly, the use of humiliation and degradation; and finally the physical torture itself.

As a doctor working for the state in St Alban's prison, I was mistrusted by those whose trust was so important. I was seen as part of the system by those whose interests I wanted to protect.

Detainees, quite understandably, are reluctant to make complaints or lay charges via the district surgeon, because they know that those complaints will be directed back to the very perpetrators of the assault. There are no independent channels for reporting assaults and no guarantee that an assault, if reported to the police, will be adequately investigated.

In the period 22 July to 16 September 1985, in North End and St Alban's prisons alone, prison documents reveal that overall 706 detainees either complained of assault or presented with injuries consistent with assault. A total of 587 detainees had injuries consistent with assault, whether or not they actually made a complaint. There is record of 434 detainees having lodged complaints of assault. Some of them did not identify the perpetrators of the assault, but some 406 identified the South African police as having been responsible. In that period we have evidence that about six or seven assaults were actually investigated. This leads me to an assumption, some questions and a challenge.

If in a period of less than two months, 406 State of Emergency detainees were allegedly assaulted by the police, in the Port Elizabeth area alone, then one can assume that there were and are thousands of assaults being perpetrated countrywide.

The questions are: Why the deafening silence? Why was I the only district surgeon to reveal these assaults? Why is Doctor Ivor Lang, who carries the burden of Steve Biko's death and the guilt of having ignored the assaults which I saw, now Chief District Surgeon in Port Elizabeth? Why have the Medical Association and the South African Medical and Dental Council not acted to bring doctors who do not report torture to task and why the apathy and lack of action from the world medical community?

My challenge to the international medical community and to the World Medical Association is to take up the issue of torture in detention and the passive role of acceptance that South African doctors play. This is an area literally asking for international pressure. That South Africa is still a member of the World Medical Association is yet another slap in the face for all detainees who are treated indifferently by doctors while in detention.

All doctors in the privileged position of providing health care to detainees should be obliged to report every incident of cruel, inhuman or degrading treatment via an independent body. It is only through pressure and sanctions that some change might be brought about in the attitude of South African medical associations and the atrocities of torture in detention revealed.

But it is not until a free, democratic, society is established in

I remained in my cell together with a number of others except for exercise time, when we all congregated in the courtyard for one hour a day. During the exercise time the names of the detainees who were to be called to Louis Le Grange police station for interrogation were called out. Throughout that week detainees were called for interrogation and returned with visible injuries and reports of assault. One came back walking with great difficulty and in great pain. He told me that he had been given 'the helicopter' which he described in bizarre detail. He showed me his bruising. The skin was broken on his waist, there were weals on his back. It was with increasing dread that I awaited my call to Louis Le Grange.

My turn came on Friday 26 July 1985. The sergeant came in together with another white security policeman. He had with him an orange quirt. The sergeant pulled out a chair and instructed me to bend over it from behind and hold myself down by clasping the underpart of the chair with my hands. I did this.

The white security Policemen then proceeded to cane me with the quirt. I was hit once or twice before falling sideways off the chair in an effort to avoid being hit. The sergeant left the room and returned with handcuffs. Strydom told him to handcuff me from behind, this was done. I was wearing a tracksuit with a hood. The sergeant pulled the hood over my head and tied the front end of the hood to my tracksuit front by means of string. This forced my head down. All I could see was the ground through a small opening. They led me to the door where I was told to wait.

I was taken to another room. I was questioned by someone, I could not see him and I did not recognise his voice. I was questioned over a number of topics while I stood there hooded and handcuffed. Whenever I denied knowledge of any of the allegations or gave an answer that did not satisfy them, I would be hit with the quirt or punched. One can hear the sound of the quirt before being hit and I would tense at the sound, expecting a blow. Sometimes there wasn't a blow. I did not know what direction it was coming from or if it would hit me at all. There is no sound prior to a punch. Suddenly without warning I would be punched. It was excruciating. Although the blows themselves were painful it was the helplessness, the disorientation, the constant tension and expectation of being hit, and the sudden unexpected blows that was the worst aspect of what I can only call torture.

From an affidavit cited by Dr Wendy Orr, recounting a detainee's experience in Port Elizabeth in 1985. The person involved was not a youth, but was said by Wendy Orr to illustrate techniques of torture widely used on detainees, including young people

South Africa that these atrocities and the aftermath thereof will be abolished for ever.

EXILE

In the great diaspora of South Africans in recent decades there have been many waves of exiles. But from 1976 the character of exiles changed – suddenly they were overwhelmingly black youths in flight from the Soweto massacre and the subsequent harassment of township children that surrounded that incident.

The terror and trauma that lie behind a child's impulsion to flee home and country are intense. But doctors, themselves in exile who work with children from South Africa and Namibia, give a glimpse into the uncharted world of exile which these children face outside the country.

But there is another new phenomenom of exile in the case of South Africa's children – internal exile. The DPSC and other witnesses spoke of the bands of uprooted children they looked after in community halls or churches, the children who hide in the bush, or in a neighbour's shed. Many children involved in organising their school or their community made the decision to vanish from their old life structures and live underground. Others, released from prison and torture, do not dare go home for fear of another experience of police raiding their home at night or, worse, of police visits which can get them branded as informers – or else of vigilante attacks. So is the small space still left for family trust and emotional coherence being eroded daily for these children in South Africa.

Escaping from apartheid

Dr Freddy Reddy, a psychiatrist in exile who works with the ANC to help children in exile

I would like to quote Frank Chikane, when he said that children born in South Africa are not allowed to be children, so that the child has to make adult decisions before he is an adult. I would like to add to that and say, that that child who makes those adult decisions, one day becomes a child again because that portion of his life has been stunted.

The child that flees into exile from South Africa today has to go through experiences which very few adults would undertake, due to the hazards and dangers that he has to face. He has no papers of identification, may be wounded through torture, depressed by losing his parents, or not giving parents information about his whereabouts, not taking farewell from his mother or his brothers and sisters. He is in flight, continuously in a state of anxiety, with heartbeats that he can't control, waiting to reach an unknown destination, not knowing whether he is going to meet friends or foes, not knowing whether he is going to be arrested by police, not knowing whether he is going to die on this journey. But finally he reaches some sort of destination.

The ANC has organised itself so that it is able today to receive most of these children and youths that are escaping from South Africa, to save their lives, to save themselves from being arrested and put into prison. When they come into our care, some of them are in a state of euphoria because they think they have reached safety and sanctuary. In the very beginning, most of them appear as if they are very happy and exhilarated, but the state changes over time. In the heat of battle, the adult takes over in this child and he is able to survive. He has no time to reflect, he has no time to understand what is happening but, in exile, when he is in a safe place he then begins to reflect. And that is when the depression, the anxiety, the fears begin to develop.

An investigation of 156 youths between the ages of 16 and 20, revealed that 81 per cent of them had existential anxiety problems. The interrelationship between people is hampered. There is a state of insecurity. Paranoia is supposed to be a symptom of illness, but in South Africa we notice through these children and youths that paranoia is a normal pattern for survival under those conditions. So we see that 81 per cent of our comrades from South Africa are living in a continuous state of insecurity.

Fifty-three per cent suffer from anxiety neurosis needing psychiatric intervention. Fifty-six per cent of those suffer from depressive type of reactions. Most of them lose their sense of concentration, have nightmares, guilt feelings, but often try to deny that these things are happening to them. The guilt feeling that they left the parents, knowing what it means in African culture leaving the parents without support, at a later stage begins to hit them. The longing for home and loved ones begins to hit them while they are trying to re-establish themselves in a new situation. The classic response is illustrated by the testimony of one young man who said 'I don't feel anything, I have no emotional reactions'.

But as time goes on, the classic reaction becomes, 'I want to go back home and change the situation. I want to go back home and fight apartheid. I want to free our people so that we may live in freedom and develop a democratic society.' But, he knows not when he will return. Six years, seven years, ten years a boy of 16 becomes a man of 26. A man of 26 falls in love. He wants to marry, he wants to have children. He wants to be a father but then suddenly, in marriage, he is unable to give the most intimate feelings to the next person. He does not know how to give love or receive love, because this whole society of South Africa has stunted the potential of the children and the parents to retain these intimate feelings of love, intimacy, joy, laughter. These have been denied these children and when they grow up they have not had the training to be able to relate to their fellow beings, let alone their spouses or their children. Many of our people both inside and outside will be having these problems in the future. And it is during these times that they re-experience all the past events in their lives, the traumatic experiences and the pains and that is when they fall ill for a second time. Outsiders are often struck by the way we laugh, we make jokes and everybody looking at us in South Africa thinks that we are a very happy people. But those laughs and jokes are deceptive. Underlying the laughter and jokes are deep and painful experiences that need to be removed.

Problems of exile

Dr Zonke Majodina, a clinical psychologist at the University of Ghana who during 18 years of exile has had much experience of working with South African and Namibian refugees

The exile experience is a rupture in a person's cultural past. The experience varies in intensity depending on a person's past history and strength of political commitment. But even when exile is considered part of the on-going political struggle, the moment of departure is nonetheless traumatic. There is then an immediate conflict between the exile's links to home and the need to integrate in the new society of his host. A feeling of transitoriness is always present. The refugee understands the need to become integrated into the whole society, but is also afraid of becoming assimilated into this new society and thus losing his South African identity. The basic conflict, stressful as it is, becomes even more intense.

To the average observer, however, the newly arrived refugee seems quite contented and in fact usually reports a sense of relief at having beaten the system. The feeling of euphoria usually lasts for some months. A conflict, however, continues and after a period is followed by a profound sense of loss of security – the emotional security of families, friends, cultural security, etc. This sense of loss is made worse if the actual physical conditions of living in the new country are difficult. Considering also that most young people have had to leave their families without informing them of their plans, the sense of loss is compounded by feelings of guilt, in the form of guilt for having abandoned comrades and relatives who have remained in South Africa and who have in turn been under constant harassment to disclose the whereabouts of the refugee. There is also the social isolation resulting from loss of friends and relatives, and which can be particularly anxiety provoking.

The entire process of exile is subjectively felt as transient and unreal. More often than not, the end result is that no real adaptation takes place in the sense of an active identification with life in the new environment. This is a fact not easily reckoned with in view of the common stereotype of refugees, that is, that they are tough, resilient people who have survived unimaginable hazards back home and have coped. Refugees themselves also perceive their job as having to cope and consider any expression of an emotional problem as a sign of failure.

At this point it is pertinent to identify who are likely to be at risk. I will mention three categories of people:

First of all, refugees are classified according to two patterns of flight – that is, anticipatory or acute. It is believed that the latter group will have greater problems. Unlike a person who has anticipated for some time the possibility of exile, the person whose departure was so precipitate that he did not have time to prepare for it will be psychologically unprepared for the exile experience.

Secondly, young people and children who are separated from their families are vulnerable.

Lastly, those who have experienced the most violence and deaths of close relatives will find it hard to have left their families behind and being uncertain what has befallen them, especially when communication with home is impossible. People who have been traumatised by torture face exile in a weakened and vulnerable psychological state and therefore with a greater risk of psychological disturbances.

I will not dwell on the kinds of emotional reactions that can be expected, as this has been already mentioned. I will only add that the anxiety, depression, paranoid behaviour, aggressiveness are collectively referred to as a social displacement syndrome or the exile syndrome, for short. Furthermore, with regard to children the term 'separation anxiety' has been used to refer to the emotional reactions observed in chidren who for one reason or

In the South African way of life, the most distressing thing is the absence of normality. Even when one restrains oneself and tries to be a pastor, it is impossible to continue to be just a pastor.

For instance, in the township of Leandra last year there was conflict. The vigilantes killed Chief Ampie Mayisa and a large number of children took refuge in Wilgespruit Fellowship Centre on the West Rand. I made a contribution in trying to take them to this place of safety.

I have never been able to get any explanation – I have never been able to devise any comforting theory – of how it came about that one day the police descended in helicopters and other vehicles on Wilgespruit and began shooting at the 80 children refugees, nor why they detained them.

My own house, with my over-80-year-old mother, was petrol bombed and the police were called. It was on a Friday. The police came on the Monday and after they had been to see what had happened on the Monday, I was told that the police said that the damage was too little and they would come again. And on the Tuesday night I woke up and saw these men in balaclavas. Within a few minutes my house was set on fire. I went to report it to the police yet again, but nothing was done about it.

As a pastor I am greatly distressed that life in South Africa is not normal. I cannot say to an ordinary person in the street – I can't say to my 80-year-old mother – that if she lives as a law-abiding citizen that the law will protect her. I can't even say to a child of 8 that so long as they are innocent the law will protect them and keep them safe.

Very Reverend Simeon Nkoane, Bishop Suffragan of Johannesburg

another are separated from their families, especially their mothers, as is the case with most children forced into exile. Such anxiety, it has been shown, predisposed a child to respond in an anti-social way to later stresses. In studies of children up to the age of 16 who have experienced separation from their families, the adverse effects observed underscore the fact that children in this age range are not emotionally mature: after all, one of the most widely accepted facts in child development is that for proper personality development to take place there has to be a framework of care and order in a child's life and there has to be continuity in the provision of these, whether by the mother or substitute care-giver.

However, when one talks about the state of separation from

family by a child in exile, it should be remembered that even inside South Africa the idea of an orderly intact family life is remote for the vast majority of black children. Displaced children, or internal refugees, have become a new phenomenon in the past two years. It is a well accepted fact also that when a child goes through overwhelmingly stressful experiences, such as this separation from family, a lot of anxiety is aroused that the child cannot cope with. This leads to disturbances of personality and a pattern of repetitive maladaptive behaviour may be set in train which in turn prevents the child from ever achieving his full potential in adult life.

The observation of these various psychological reactions to the exile syndrome is in accord with the psycho-social theory of illness which states that people exposed to stressful social environmental experiences have adverse mental health, social functioning and physical health. There are of course differences to be found from person to person and these are based on two factors: first, the degree to which a person perceives others as providing social support; secondly, the maturity of his coping skills and, as I've just said, children are not mature enough to cope successfully.

Particularly relevant here are studies conducted among exiles. Without exception findings indicate that people who are in exile have poorer physical and psychological health status than comparison populations. This should not be particularly surprising to those of us in exile, but perhaps what escapes our notice is the fact that children and adolescents are more vulnerable. I conducted a survey on a small random sample of adolescent Namibian refugee students studying in Ghana. They are students who have been in Ghana for the past year or two — they are all members of SWAPO and are sponsored by the United Nations High Commission for Refugees. In trying to facilitate their adjustment to Ghanaian society they are placed in different schools all over the country and come back to Accra, the capital, during holidays.

To measure anxiety status the 20 students were asked to fill in a structured questionnaire consisting of 54 statements to which they had to answer 'yes' or 'no'. Analysis of the completed questionnaires show that anxiety level among the students was higher than is usually seen in adolescents of their age. The prevalence of specific symptoms such as headaches, stomach aches and generally bodily pains in general ranged from 90 to 100 per cent. Statements relating to unhappiness, feelings of sadness, loneliness, of being preoccupied with events at home were next in

99

frequency. In fact, almost all of them answered 'yes' to the item: other children are happier than I am.

Similar findings could be expected from South African children forced into exile. This study was conducted on adolescents and one significant feature of this age is that all adolescents go through the otherwise normal developmental task of establishing a sense of personal identity. For the young person in exile, the problem of creating a meaningful sense of identity is not much different from that faced by his counterpart inside South Africa. Both have to draw on the past identifications they have been making with significant people, situations and experiences right from early childhood – that is, models in the social environment.

And what kind of social environment is the young South African black child familiar with? The violence of apartheid, with its racism, with its injustices, its disruption of family life, its inferior and distorted education, inhuman living conditions, denial of basic human rights and the present endless State of Emergency. From all this the young person must emerge with a personal identity and a set of values, but can anyone meaningfully identify with an inferior status, with being discriminated against, with being a third-class citizen, with economic underprivilege, with a character where he is expected to be submissive, with a lack of control over his destiny and with uncertainty prevailing over his life all the time? No wonder, then, that the average black youth rejects all of this but, by so doing, he is likely to be thrown into a state of personal disequilibrium commonly referred to as a crisis of identity.

This crisis of identity suffered by most black youths inside and outside the country highlights the fact that both political repression and exile tend to distort the normal development of socialisation in a child or young person. Both can lead to a sense of ambivalence which may inhibit creative potential. Most of the time the young person identifies with the cause that has most meaning for him: the struggle to dismantle apartheid. But optimism about the struggle can become a cover for an underlying psychological vulnerability. It usually takes a lot of critical self-examination for the young person to understand himself and to achieve a sense of realistic purpose.

What can be done about these problems children face in exile? How can we develop a strategy that will not only confront the problems but also make itself part of the process of personal growth and development in these children? I am concerned with how best we in the exile community can use our resources to help. It will be useful, for example, to consider a community-based

100

mental health programme and the Solomon Mahlangu Freedom College at Mazimbu would be the right kind of setting to start with in view of the infrastructure laid down by the ANC there. From testimonies given by various professionals who work there, it is obvious that they have to grapple daily with some of the psychological problems already mentioned. According to one nursing sister attached to the nursery school, there are many problems in looking after the nursery school children, especially those who have been separated from their refugee parents and who find it difficult to accept their separation. Some react by withdrawing from other children, others have nightmares, while others are aggressive or have emotional outbursts of crying and anger. What the children need more than anything else is a relationship with adults who will assume a parental responsibility. Because of the separation they have experienced, they need people who will guarantee unconditional affection and support and who will have a good deal of understanding and patience.

When the United Democratic Front was launched in South Africa in August 1983 as a coalition of grassroots organisations of widely varying political hues, but linked by a common rejection of apartheid, the depth of organisation these modest church, community and other groups had already achieved was not widely appreciated. But when the state began to react by unleashing its repressive forces many of the UDF organisations proved unexpectedly resilient. New layers of organisation emerged as the leadership was detained, or in some cases murdered. The National Education Crisis Committee (NECC), whose message to the conference is printed below, was formed as part of this process. The fact that the organisation sent the message when all but one of its executive was in detention, and that one in hiding, is a measure of what a high priority the democratic movement puts on breaking the power of censorship by speaking outside South Africa whenever possible.

The rejection of apartheid education has been one of the main factors in the mobilisation of resistance, and an issue which has played a key role in uniting children with the rest of the community in organised struggle over a whole range of issues. Rent and consumer boycotts, stay- aways from work and boycotts of the apartheid education system have all contributed to a united expression of the rejection of apartheid, and of the determination of the majority of South Africans to change the conditions under which apartheid forces them to live.

Women organisers like Cynthia Tinto and Pauline Moloise illustrate the unstinting support of the mothers behind this new generation of black children who, as the Reverend Finca describes them below, are 'the children who can not adjust to apartheid'.

Education as a Liberation Force

Read to the conference in Molobi's absence as a statement by the National Education Crisis Committee. Molobi, in hiding at the time of the conference, was detained three months later, in December

For entire communities, especially young children who must still grow to life under the system of apartheid, let this conference act as a pillar of hope and a fountain of encouragement. It is our wish that they may begin to see the light at the end of the tunnel more clearly. As someone once said, no lie can live forever.

In South Africa, education has always been a malleable tool in the hands of the white racist majority. The architects of Bantu education openly declared that the education of the black person must be in consonance with the overall political policies of their government. Even if they were to deny it, the very fabric of South African society bears glaring witness to those intentions.

Whole communities have been separated from each other, children have been brought up in glaringly unequal, oppressive, hideous conditions. Black children have been robbed of whole life opportunities, exposed to an education system whose basic aim was to keep them barely conscious of their human worth and dignity. The very books prescribed in schools show this. From the earliest ages of their schooling, they are given subject material full of references to rural and tribal settings. In the pre-1976 revolt era, the intentions were clearly to teach all other subjects, especially the sciences, through the medium of Afrikaans. This trend has not stopped.

The bad effects of apartheid education do not affect only the black child. White education for white children is equally bad. These children, coming from socially privileged but acutely secluded lives, are taken through a system which not only distorts their conceptions of the black school child's world, but also through calculated omissions, also deprives them of the fuller understanding of their country. The white child grows up with negative stereotypes which are strengthened by the regimes's policies. In the media, he or she internalises lies, distortions, political propaganda aimed at protecting racial superiority. The worst and unfortunate thing for that child, is the day he is called up to don the SADF uniform, when he has to take up arms against other children in the townships. Here he is thrown into a mental make-up of the so-called national security. He realises that, in order to protect the white nation, he must protect his own skin in the face of thousands of angry black children. He resorts to the gun, to the destruction of lives, he becomes a schizophrenic because he can't cope with the double life he is called upon to live: the glossy life of his parents and white communities, the life of success, of big business, of quiet suburbia and green luxurious gardens, against that of black bleeding bodies that die in township debris.

Education cannot be viewed in isolation from other forces at play in society. In all societies where ownership of the means of production and access to the proceeds of that productive system is based on class, color or creed, or a combination of any of these, those who dominate always ensure that the state and the entire

One of the fundamental events that has taken place in South Africa in the past decade and a half is that there has been born in our land a new generation of black children. Children who cannot adjust to apartheid. I remember as a young boy I had my share of what I thought was the struggle against apartheid in debates and debating societies in the school room, but my children are born into a completely new environment. From the moment they are born they are confronted by two simple choices: one is to adjust to living as second-class persons in apartheid, the other choice is to die in a bitter and ugly fight against apartheid.

Friends, between these two there is no middle ground. As far as the young people of South Africa are concerned, you are either engaged in the bitter struggle to fight against apartheid, or you are not. Adjusting to or participating in any other way in the life of South Africa is considered to be conforming to apartheid.

This has led to two reactions. The first one is that the perpetrators of apartheid have focused mainly on young people as targets and I'm going to draw upon a few examples from the Border region from which I come.

At King Williamstown . . . in a school called Nobendulo young children were rounded up by the police, put in a hippo and dumped into the Buffalo River. Six children died on the spot. In the report in the *Daily Dispatch* the following day it was reported 'Six Terrorists Killed in the Buffalo River' and that the reason for what happened was that whilst the police were doing their duty of maintaining law and order these children were found to be obstructing law and order.

At Duncan Village in East London a 5-year-old child was playing in the street. He was shot by the so-called security police. It was reported that a 5-year-old had been shot because the police were defending themselves: a 5-year-old was a threat to the security of the state.

In Queenstown a 14-year-old was sentenced to 5 years' imprisonment and kept in a cell with adult long-term prisoners. The sexual molestation he suffered has had a devastating effect on his total life. He can never be the same again.

I can go on and on, but I just want to add that the University of Fort Hare is today more of a concentration camp than a centre for university education.

There is another effect of the repression. Instead of making our young people docile, it is making them more and more angry and ruthless. I want to make this appeal, that when the people from the free world condemn us, they should remember they have not felt what it is like to be born and grow and live in Duncan Village

104

or in Mdantsane or in Zwelitsha or in Ginsberg. They must think twice before they condemn us.

Reverend Blessings Finca, a pastor of the Reformed Presbyterian Church and Chairperson of the Border Council of Churches. Shortly after his return from the Harare Conference he was taken in for questioning by the Ciskei bantustan security police and questioned about the conference

cultural apparatus are attuned to their continued domination. The present crisis in education, and the heavy-handed manner in which the South African regime has reacted to the crisis, must both be seen against the backdrop of relations within South African society. It is clear that the white minority has used education as an integral part of oppression. If the oppressed, in their attempt to shake off their chains of oppression, trample over the gutter system of apartheid education, they are reacting to a reality and are within their democratic right. Oppression is a painful and abnormal situation, freedom is a legitimate normality justifiable for all human beings.

The story of our people's resistance against apartheid is a well-known one. The struggle for a better education system in South Africa goes a long way back to the days of colonialism. When the colonizer came, he was repulsed by the people. Through the sheer might of his sophisticated gun-power he managed to force his settlement on the land. The introduction of slave education was resisted by the chiefs. When Bantu education was forced upon our communities in 1954, teachers and pupils resisted, the boycott method was used. Some of the teachers were forced to resign, many joined industry while others were forced into exile.

The South African regime did not stop. In the pursuance of the bantustan policies, separate universities were established. Those colleges are now the very cutting edge of struggle in education today. SADF and SAP presence in them is on a daily basis. Students must pursue education confronted by the barrel of the gun. In the mid-seventies, the student uprisings of 1976 were a culmination of decades of resistance against a rotten system of education. Hundreds of students were shot, some of those children went missing leaving no trace at all and have never been heard from again.

In the 1980s the student movement grew in leaps and bounds. The birth of COSAS saw the galvanisation of thousands upon thousands of students. The aspirations of students became clearer

105

Amandla! Freedom. I am a wife of a detainee, Christmas Tinto. He was the first vice-president of the Western Cape UDF when the State of Emergency was declared in June 1986. He had to go into hiding because he feared that he would be detained. He was in hiding for seven months. Unfortunately in January this year the security police caught him while he was visiting me, because I had a baby in January. He has since been in detention and he is still in detention now. The anger of wives who have to bear the problem of bringing up children alone because the father is in detention is great. Sometimes we have problems as women, mothers and fathers, becoming divided, because we sometimes blame one another when a child is detained.

Our children are the flowers of our struggle and the principal reason for our fight. As mothers, we should fully support our kids in every field of our struggle. Our kids are being termed criminals by the state. Even in political cases arising out of campaigns against the community councils and the consumer boycotts, they are being criminalised. When we see our children in the docks, it becomes unbearable psychologically and physically and you blame yourself, because you think why don't these people detain me instead of detaining my child?

Cynthia Tinto, a member of the United Women's Congress in Cape Town

and sharper. When in 1984, the Vaal complex exploded in rent boycotts that were to sweep through the country, the state, through its overstretched police apparatus was facing an obviously worsening situation of mass resistance and had no choice but to adopt even harsher methods of repression. The State of Emergency was declared, thousands of people, many of them schoolchildren were detained. The regime had started its decline. Only naked repression could save it. Naked repression is still its only hope. Today, we can say that the naked repression that has become our normal life is a clear indication of the failure of apartheid. The regime is blind to negotiations and the so-called reform is a lie. The intransigent nature of the South African regime can be seen precisely in the field of education.

Shortly after the first State of Emergency and the banning of COSAS, a group of parents, priests and teachers were called together in what is known as the Soweto Parents Crisis Committee (SPCC). This committee was mandated to initiate discussions with the Department of Education and Training (DET) with the aim of resolving an explosive schooling situation. At the time a great number of children had already lost their lives. Some were maimed. The entire schooling system was grinding to a halt. The DET, which was later joined by the Department of Law and Order, met the communities' requests with a negative attitude. Nothing was gained from those discussions.

Subsequently, at a National Conference, the National Education Crisis Committee was formed to co-ordinate educational programmes on a national scale. It was immediately after the NECC leadership had held discussions with these Departments of the government that almost all of them were detained. Some of these people, in fact most of them, are still in detention. These people were thrown into detention for actually challenging the state talks. Today the same regime pretends to the outside world that it seeks to talk. All these detentions of schoolchildren, teachers and parents, happened after these people had discussed and agreed that in 1986 the schoolchildren would return to school. Not even this indication of goodwill would satisfy this regime locked in acute crisis. In fact, the detentions, the repression and the propaganda about reform are a smokescreen hiding the real crisis and failures of apartheid. After the detentions of pupils, teachers, parents and the leadership of the NECC, this is what happened.

1. A system of identity cards similar in intent to passes was introduced at schools.
2. Army presence in school yards continued.
3. There was a vehement refusal to change the curriculum.
4. Teachers who were popular with students were transferred to far-off places without consent or negotiation.
5. People's education materials were banned.
6. NECC meetings were banned and there was a campaign of raiding NECC offices all over the country. This followed new detentions of NECC activists and students.
7. The government introduced what they called 'study camps' which were rejected by students as propaganda centres.

This programme of detentions and harassment is complemented by an elaborate national programme of systematic repression. The systematic clamp-down includes new, stringent censorship legislation being passed on the media and new, strict regulations reasserting state policy and security on universities, schools, colleges. The introduction of Regional Service Councils and Joint Management Centres meant tighter control of local affairs by government. Evictions of families and communities intensified with obvious disruptive effect on organisations. Scores of political

I was taught by my son, and eventually I thought that really he's telling the truth, it is not time for tears. When I started crying he used to ask me, 'Why are you crying?', ' What happened?' 'What's the matter?' Then if I said I feel pity for him, then he used to say 'Look, there isn't any time for tears. It's time now for joy, because now really people are awakening. People should be awakening. If you sit in that corner and start crying you are doing nothing. Mummy, you go out and go in joy. Stop sitting like an old lady crying, feeling sorry and pity for me. You don't have to pity me.' So, I'm also trying to convince the other mothers that have got children on Death Row that they mustn't cry, they must always think and always pray that one day something is going to happen.

Pauline Moloise whose son Benjamin was executed by the apartheid regime on 18 October 1985, in defiance of world opinion and an unprecedented number of calls for clemency. He had been convicted for the killing of a security policeman in 1982, an act he always denied and for which the ANC claimed responsibility, stating that Moloise was not involved. Since then Pauline Moloise has been active in the campaigns to save others who have been sentenced to death in the repression of resistance.

A 6-year-old boy said to me 'Just watch me jump. I jump very high, eh?' I said to him 'Ja', but I wasn't paying any particular interest and he kept on insisting that I should watch how he jumps. And I said to him 'But why are you insisting?' He says 'One has to jump high because prison walls are high.' I said to him 'Now, do you think you are going to prison?' He said to me 'Yes, I'm going to prison.' I said to him 'Why?' He said 'Because I'm a comrade, and tell the children to come outside. I tell the teacher I'm going to the toilet and I call the children out and I teach them to toi-toi (do the freedom dance) so they're going to put me in prison.'

A teacher in the Western Cape

trials with dozens of people waiting on Death Row to be hanged similarly attacked the roots of organisations within the townships. Recently there have been moves to arm more heavily the bantustan leaders who have already a harrowing record of excesses with regard to activists and opponents of apartheid.

One of the very disturbing developments in recent South Africa is the rising number of activists who no longer die in detention, but become victims of a vicious campaign of vigilante death squads. Murders by men clad in balaclavas who sow death by night are a common phenomenon today. None of these murderers are apprehended, yet police detain activists by the score.

This is the crisis of apartheid. This is the acute bankruptcy of a political system on the way out. Our people are not convinced that such a system can be reformed, nor can Bantu education.

Our conviction is that we must place the building blocks of a new South African person. We in the NECC talk of a people's education system upon whose foundation an emancipated South Africa will blossom. By people's education, we envisage a democratic education system which will break down the mystifying walls which surround elitist education. We strongly believe that no democratic education system can be developed in an undemocratic political system. Democracy requires conditions conducive to its practice and survival. We foresee an education system which will call for the involvement of parents as workers and academics, parents as people sharing their expertise. We foresee an education system which will balance learning and production. Our vision is that of an education system which will produce an enquiring mind, not only receptive, but also open to the needs of our whole society.

We have to start from where we are now. That is a society torn apart by conflict, a conflict between those who stand for the preservation of apartheid against the rest of the population – freedom-loving people who struggle for a free non-racial and democratic future South Africa.

People's education has of course taken the side of the people. People's education stands with the hopes of a future South Africa. People's education therefore is part of the liberating process. Change is a force that works both ways. We are willing to be moulded by the process of change as we work for social change. We call upon academics in South Africa to become part of this two-fold change. They must be changed too. They must form a unified block decidedly on the side of the people. For too long they have been tools helpful to big capital and therefore directly or indirectly limited to the forces of oppression. As the contradictions in South Africa sharpen, they will continue to find it more difficult to continue their ivory tower, individualist, existence. We in the communities, in the labour movement, in the schools, are saying it is not enough to write highfaluting theories about us, get doctorates in the process, and become so-called experts on this or that organisation or field, to develop your scathing critiques

During the late sixties and early seventies (which many people regard as the dark ages in the political history of our people), draconian measures were introduced by the apartheid regime, such as the 90-day detention laws, the 180-day detention laws, culminating in the notorious Section 6 of the Terrorism Act. This was an attempt to counter the campaign of limited sabotage that had been mounted by the liberation movements in the early sixties. The effect was that our people started becoming afraid. People began fearing their own shadows. But in the early seventies the black people of South Africa began to rediscover themselves and they looked deep into themselves, into their heritage. Inspired by the teachings of their compatriots, both inside and outside the country, and by the examples of others in Africa, Europe and in America, they cast off fear and regained their self-respect. This resurgence culminated in the action of young people of 16 June 1976 and after. This day, 16 June, has a very special place in the history of South Africa in general and of its children in particular. On that day, as everybody knows, unarmed students in Soweto were mowed down by armed policemen.

This event sparked off massive resistance which spread to the rest of the country. The acts of brutal repression witnessed by 6, 7 and 8-year-olds were implanted deeply in their psyche. South Africa has never forgotten that day. The children of South Africa have not forgotten that day. The 6, 7 and 8-year-olds of 1976 are now the youths of today. What they have witnessed and suffered has made them adults in a very short time.

The children of South Africa have taken a decision that they will be free. They have organised themselves so effectively that their organisation, COSAS, was banned in 1985. Undetered by this, they have re-organised themselves.The children believe that they owe no allegiance to this regime because it is not based on the will of the governed but on brutal force. They have not accepted the banning of what they consider the people's organisation, they publicly chant and sing praises of those they regard as the real leaders of the people. They have displayed the banned flags and insignia in full view of the police.

Marumo Statsi Moerane, a Durban Advocate

from the safe walls and desks of your professions, and thereby hope to gain acceptance or recognition in our daily struggles. As the cutting edge of struggle becomes sharper, the call is for you to soil your gowns with work for a future South Africa. At the end of

110

the day, it is not only your views, but also your contribution that tells on which side you are.

The challenge facing our structures in South Africa is that of organising. We must organise and organise yet again. We must build our structures. So must the academics and intellectuals in their domains.

Two experts on international law brought to Harare a different perspective on the testimony of the children. The daily violence of the system against them, the laws which deprive the majority of South Africans of their basic rights, the actions of the Minister of Law and Order whose power loomed so threateningly, were all subjected to the test of higher laws.

According to the international law on human rights, these experts argued, apartheid and its practices – in particular the treatment of children – involve crimes against humanity.

Apartheid and Genocide

Kader Asmal, Dean of Arts, Trinity College, Dublin, and an expert in International Law

The planned, systematic extermination on racial, ethnic or national grounds of entire human groups such as Jews, Gypsies or Slavs, were treated as criminal acts by the Statute of London and the Nuremberg Tribunal. The concept of 'crimes against humanity' has come into use in the international legal vocabulary as a direct result of the racialist and totalitarian practices based in particular on fascism and nazism. These barbaric acts were the impetus for the adoption of the Convention on the Prevention and Punishment of the Crime of Genocide in 1948.

The Nuremberg War Crimes Tribunal in 1946 saw the first international legal illustration of the use of the word 'genocide' in the indictment constituting crimes against humanity. The General Assembly of the United Nations in resolution (96 (1) 1946) which confirmed the Nuremberg Principles as part of international law laid down that the crime of genocide could occur independently of war crimes or a war of aggression. The violation of the right to life on an extensive and concentrated scale by the apartheid regime, the violations of the physical and mental integrity of the black population, especially through mass removals and deportations, the collective removal of citizenship and the adoption of administrative and economic policies which result in large-scale and early deaths of children have been integral parts of the policy of apartheid. Most important, the apartheid system denies the vast majority of the population of South Africa the right to nationhood and denies cultural, linguistic and social autonomy to them.

The association between the crime of apartheid and genocide

has been thereby drawn out by a recent report of an Ad Hoc
Working Group of Experts appointed by the UN Commission on
Human Rights, which details the effects of apartheid, both from
the point of view of the 'orthodox' approach to genocide and the
broader interpretation 'to mean any act calculated to destroy the
individual or prevent him from participating fully in national
life,' which would embrace 'political, economic and social life'.

This report is the first full review of the genocidal policy of the
South African regime. The Report's findings are also applicable to
Namibia. The Report notes that 'all the criteria used to define the
crime of genocide coincide with the definition of a crime against
humanity.' Apartheid is, therefore, 'not simply a crime against
humanity but a series of acts of genocide, as far as some aspects of
its practices and policies are concerned, but also with implica-
tions for international peace and security'.

This United Nations Report concluded with an important
appeal:

> The South African regime should thus be seen in a new
> light. Accordingly, we consider that the competent
> United Nations bodies could usefully draw the atten-
> tion of the international community to this new hidden
> aspect of apartheid, which is insidiously assuming a
> number of forms of genocide – in both the strict and
> broader meanings of the term.
>
> The leaders of the apartheid regime and those who
> carry out illegal orders are responsible for their actions.
> A free and democratic State of South Africa could use
> the precedent of the Nuremberg Trials to discharge its
> duty under international law by punishing them for
> crimes against humanity and other crimes in interna-
> tional law.
>
> But the outrages against children also require a
> response from the international community. There is a
> duty not to assist in the perpetration of criminal action.
> Those who are committed to removing such illegal
> actions need to be assisted. The outrages against black
> children cannot be treated complacently. They would
> not be treated in such a cavalier fashion if the children
> had been white. Such treatment is a blot on the
> international community and must be speedily
> removed. Only then can the children of South Africa
> receive the benefits of the standards established by
> international law.

Targetting the Children of South Africa: A New Crime of State

Richard Falk, Professor of International Law and Practice at Princeton University. This is an expanded version of his contribution to the conference

I

In a century filled with many atrocities, there is no need to claim a special status for apartheid. At the same time there is a special moral claim present: this form of acute repression is intensifying and is likely to produce massive suffering throughout the whole of South Africa before it collapses. And for Americans this claim has added dimensions. The United States continues to play a complicit role, helping to sustain the South African economy and indirectly lending support to the Pretoria regime.

The moral quality of a government is disclosed by the way it treats those subject to its power who are the most vulnerable and the most innocent. And we also generally agree that the child best symbolises conditions of vulnerability and innocence. We are particularly shocked by private crimes against children, and regard public abuse of children even in wartime as horror in its purest form. Often the child as victim of war comes to express an overall sense of tragedy. For many people, the widely displayed news photo of a Vietnamese child, her body aflame, running away from a napalm attack, came to symbolise the core meaning of the Vietnam war.

Similarly, the vicious repression of children in South Africa has made the inner logic of apartheid more transparent than it has ever been before. It had become evident that the South African state has been systematically engaged in battle with the children of the townships, relying on modern weaponry to offset a massive and spontaneous resistance movement. In this setting, the black African child has gained prominence both for being victimised and for being at the centre of a heroic movement of resistance.

Apartheid has survived partly because the government of South Africa is white, Western and considered a geo-political asset when it comes to East-West matters. Americans, with their own unfinished agenda of anti-racism, should rank this struggle their highest moral and political priority. To be fully human in the last part of this century means to be engaged actively in the struggle to destroy apartheid.

II

There is always something bewildering about invoking law in relation to apartheid. The South African government has relied upon a kind of ultra-legalism to give form and substance to the specific content of apartheid. As such, in the lives of South Africans, law, apartheid and racial discrimination operate as interchangeable realities. The legal order has become an instrument of severe injustice, and what the state considers 'lawlessness' has come to be the indispensable posture for those who want to act with any decency, even if they limit their activities to non-violent opposition. Even the advocacy of multiracial democracy and an end to apartheid can be and has been frequently prosecuted under South African 'security legislation', whether it be the Terrorism Act or the Suppression of Communism Act in the past or the Internal Security Act of today.

But there is fortunately more to the content of law than the official acts of the Pretoria government. There exists a law that binds governments and gives individuals and groups a clear sense as to the outer limits of governmental authority. If a government deliberately flouts international law and inflicts serious harm on its own citizenry, then it is guilty of Crimes against Humanity. If these crimes persist, rights of resistance emerge. In the South African case the system of apartheid is an ongoing criminal enterprise that has brazenly refused to heed the legal censure of the entire world as expressed in binding pronouncements from various organs of the United Nations Organisation. It is this second sense of law that condemns apartheid, that informs this discussion of the rights of children.

Until recent decades the individual was almost effaced from the protective gaze of international law. Only states were deemed subjects of rights and duties. As a result, given the territorial arrangement of state power, governments were legally free to abuse their own populations. Only foreigners were protected, because to do harm to an alien was to do wrong to his or her state, giving rise to a state claim. In this regard, the very idea of an international law of human rights is subversive of the traditional idea of state sovereignty. It insinuates claims on behalf of individuals that can be directed against alleged abuses of state power, and thereby erodes the purity of territorial sovereignty and establishes a legal basis for insisting that all government be responsive to international (to the organised world community) and to transnational (to voluntary organisations and public opinion) accountability.

One of the most impressive achievements since World War II is the development of an international law of human rights, starting with the Universal Declaration of Human Rights (1948), moving into the Genocide Convention (1948), and then to the Covenant on Civil and Political Rights and the Covenant on Social and Economic Rights (1966), and finally, leading to the International Convention on the Elimination of All Forms of Racial Discrimination (1966). These documents have been drafted under the auspices of the United Nations and reflect a broad consensus on standards of conduct that transcend the fissures of East and West, North and South. They provide us with a body of authoritative standards against which to measure complaints about the abuse of state power. Governments can no longer contend, as had been the case, that treatment of their citizenry is an internal matter of policy and judgment. These legal instruments have by now been entered into the corpus of general international law, and are binding whether or not a particular government accords its formal assent.

The great achievement of this post-1945 build-up of an international law of human rights is to advance the process of establishing agreed global standards for the behaviour of governments toward individuals and groups. Unfortunately, the existence of these standards does not imply their acceptance in practice. And what is more, procedures for implementing and enforcing these standards are almost entirely absent on an international level. The most that can be done in the face of gross and persistent violations is to mobilise international public opinion, and to activate procedures that withdraw legitimacy from a particular government. It is a particular challenge to concerned people, voluntary associations, and like-minded governments to call attention to this South African campaign of repression against township children. Often publicising atrocities has political consequences. As information becomes power in our wired media-hyped world, telling this particular story of human abuse improves the prospects for stronger sanctions against South Africa, as well as adding to the overall effort to deny the apartheid regime its claim to legitimacy and sovereign rights whenever the issue presents itself, whether it's a matter of participating in South African sporting activities or insisting that an organisation divest itself of investments tainted by their connections with apartheid.

The larger claim is that the United Nations system by itself seems unable to promote an effective anti-apartheid police, and that the peoples of the world have an opportunity, as well as an obligation, to take necessary and proper actions on their own initiative. It is part of a wider realisation that the playing fields of democracy are less territorial and nationalistic than previously, and more transnational. Many private initiatives disclose both the reality of an international dimension of struggle, but also the difficulty of achieving results. A ruthless, determined government, even if supported only by a minority, can be exceedingly difficult to dislodge from power. At the very least, the normative situation has been clarified by the existence of widely accepted minimum standards in the context of human rights and race relations, but to make the behaviour of governmental violators conform to these standards remains a formidable challenge, one that is addressed to all of us.

III

Our preoccupation with the protection of children is of recent origin. As one specialist on children, Lloyd Demause, notes (in *The History of Childhood*): 'The history of childhood is a nightmare from which we have only recently begun to awaken. The further back in history one goes, the lower the level of child care, and the more likely children are to be killed, abandoned, beaten, terrorised, and sexually abused.' Societal practices associated with infanticide and sacrifice, especially of female children, were widespread in pre-modern times, continued late into the last century and have not altogether disappeared from many local settings in the contemporary world. More common in recent times is disregard of children as individuals, allowing parents, teachers and employers an almost unlimited authority to treat children as private property, subject to physical and sexual abuse, and to being sold in the market as slaves or prostitutes. In the modern era, until social welfare attitudes shifted, rights of contract enabled employers to use child labour for nominal wages and with no responsibility for health and safety.

In this century there has been a growing international recognition that children are vulnerable, innocent victims of societal practices that can be cruel and harmful to proper human development. The principal international concern has been to prohibit societal abuses of children by traditional practices and to establish standards for basic needs so that children will be able to enter adulthood with the basis for a productive life.

International efforts along these lines began with the Geneva Declaration of the Rights of the Child of 1924. This special focus on children was carried forward in the Declaration of the Rights of the Child adopted in 1959. In the preamble the spirit of the

117

undertaking was expressed by the now famous phrase, ' mankind owes to the child the best it has to give.'

Further recognition of the duty to protect the child is found in statutes and formal pronouncements of several specialised agencies within the United Nations family, especially of Unicef.

The most significant effort at standard-setting is undoubtedly the Draft Convention on the Rights of the Child that has been under preparation for several years, following an initial Polish initiative in 1981 within the setting of the UN Commission on Human Rights. As earlier, the basic effort is to assure that children will be protected from the sort of abuses that have interfered in the past with their positive development. But significantly at the 1986 session of the Working Group assigned to prepare a final draft of this Convention, a new Article 19 was proposed that is directly responsive to the circumstances that exist in South Africa where children, as such, are habitually treated as enemies of the state. The text of Article 19 is an important contribution to the development of international law bearing on the situation of children even though as yet it has not been formally incorporated in the Convention and the Convention itself has not been adopted.[*Details of the UN Declaration of the Rights of the Child and of provisions of Article 19 of the Draft Convention, will be found in Appendix II*]

The patterns of practice by South African security forces since 1976 have involved the most flagrant possible disregard of the legal rules set forth for adoption in Article 19, especially as relating to conditions of detention and overall duties to take special account of the family unit when the alleged criminal offender is a child. Such a legal mandate is strengthened in this instance by the character of the detention and charges being associated with active opposition to a system of racial oppression that has itself been authoritatively declared by the United Nations to be a Crime against Humanity.

Closely related is the recent addition to the draft convention of the three-part Article 20 calling for application of international humanitarian law to children caught up in armed conflict, a new concern relating, in part, to the situation in Southern Africa. The prohibition in the second paragraph of the proposed article asserts an obligation to 'refrain in particular from recruiting children into the armed forces' and requires states to 'take all feasible measures to ensure that children do not take part in hostilities.'

This Draft Convention on the Rights of the Child offers the prospect of a framework on the international legal level for assessing whether a government is behaving adequately in

118

relation to children within its reach. It will probably take some years before this Draft Convention comes into force as a treaty, and it is virtually assured that the current South African government will refuse to become a party. Nevertheless, if widely adhered to, and generally in keeping with the 1959 Declaration of the Rights of the Child and of the wider protective framework of the international law of human rights, this new convention will help to pinpoint South Africa's campaign of abuse against township children, and its obligatory force will be universal in scope. By now, international legal experts agree that a widely endorsed multilateral treaty that deals with normative issues possesses a legislative effect, that it becomes binding for the entire community, including non-participating states.

Such a campaign of abuse, now widely documented as taking place over a period of years and in the face of many protests by human rights groups, seems to constitute a separate criminal undertaking within the understanding of international law. Since the Nuremberg Judgment government officials are potentially responsible as individuals for Crimes against Humanity. This category of offence is specified in Principle VI(c) of the Nuremberg Principles as formulated by the International Law Commission:

> Murder, extermination, enslavement, deportation and other inhuman acts done against any civilian popula-
> tion, or persecution on political, racial or religious grounds, when such acts are done or such persecutions are carried on in execution of or in connection with any crime against peace or any war crime.

It is arguable that positive international law no longer requires that the inhuman acts be connected with war or crimes against peace, but even if this requirement endures, it seems satisfied by the sporadic warfare carried on by South Africa against the Front Line States, undertakings involving both aggressive force – crimes against the peace – and wrongful conduct in combat – war crimes.

Without entering into detailed discussion of the patterns of detention, torture, terror, and prolonged confinement associated with the campaign against the children, it seems evident that the South African government is in flagrant and continuing violation of international law and that its policy-makers are potentially subject to criminal prosecution.

119

My contact with the US Embassy in Harare was not reassuring. Unlike many other resident diplomats, the US Ambassador watched events disinterestedly from the sidelines, self-consciously distancing himself. After a particularly moving session at the conference the second-ranking US diplomat, a pleasant, experienced Foreign Service officer, told me, 'If I listened to speeches like that for three days, my head would turn to mush.' Perhaps, at this stage, a little mush of this sort would improve the quality of US policy in the region.

Richard Falk, recalling his contact in Harare with his own embassy

IV

We are all challenged to act urgently on behalf of these South African children. It is evident that a courageous struggle of resistance goes on within South Africa. It is evident that foreign governments are moving away from full normal diplomatic and economic relations with Pretoria, but are mainly not ready to support actively the liberation struggle. The United Nations provides moral suasion, legal assessment, and the auspices for collective measures when the political climate is so disposed.

Even in the setting of a widely endorsed liberation struggle, this formal action against apartheid by governments and international institutions, while necessary, is unlikely to be sufficient to bring change in the years ahead. There are additional opportunities for private initiatives to advance the struggle, especially by building pressure for disinvestment and sanctions at the regional and international level, undertaking of great relevance within Great Britain and the United States.

Because South Africa perverts law in the course of legalising 'apartheid' within South Africa it is especially important to reclaim law for the purposes of social justice and the defence of rights. Such a process of reclaiming can proceed from two directions: resistance within the country and opposition from without. In both instances, international law as it has evolved, validates these anti-apartheid claims, and permits law to be reclaimed by the people of South Africa and elsewhere as an instrument of their struggle. This is a signal achievement, and of great potential political significance.

The indication of the legitimacy of government may be most clearly disclosed by how a government treats those who are most disadvantaged within its population. The child, no matter how

120

badly treated in the past, has emerged in this century as the prime expression of societal self- regard. South Africa's campaign against township children waged with an unremitting fury for more than a decade must be appreciated, then, as a direct assault on this common element of human decency that has been enshrined in the emergent international law bearing on the rights of the child.

The struggle against apartheid has become the first shared global enterprise on behalf of human rights and in opposition to official racism. It has received formal support from all elements of international society. The way we respond as individuals and societies to the international call to end apartheid tests our humanity in this last portion of the century in a manner that is true of no other issue. We can no longer turn away without ourselves suffering adverse consequences.

Developments since Harare

The organisers and convenors of the conference can undoubtedly claim that the conference had an impact both inside South Africa and outside.

While it was being held and shortly thereafter the Minister of Law and Order, Adriaan Vlok, took several steps to counter the information being disseminated from the conference and to undercut its impact. On 23 September he issued a press release in which he claimed that there were only 115 children under 17 in detention and not thousands as was alleged by the DPSC. He claimed that they were held in connection with serious offences and that their detention was 'absolutely necessary'. Within a week of the conference ending he saw fit to release 41 of these detainees. The DPSC denied that they had claimed that thousands of children were then in detention, but they did claim that the Minister had been deceptive in refusing to release the total number of under-18-year-olds in detention (18 being the age that the law itself uses to classify persons as children) while the Minister had arbitrarily chosen the age of 17. In the same week, the South Africa Prison Service staged a soccer tournament for child detainees and had the exercise filmed by the South African Broadcasting Corporation. The Johannesburg newspapers the *Weekly Mail* and the *New Nation* labelled these as propaganda exercises designed to pre-empt or undercut the findings of the Harare Conference. Indeed Adriaan Vlok himself stated that the 'propaganda' spread at the conference was 'causing South Africa untold damage'. The DPSC has acknowleged a shift in the pattern of detentions with fewer persons being detained under the Emergency Regulations.

At the end of the conference, delegates agreed to take the issue back to their different countries or their professional associations. One such group of professionals, the lawyers, resolved to form an international association of lawyers against apartheid. When the Commonwealth Heads of Government met in Vancouver in October they were 'deeply disturbed' by evidence from the conference and called upon Pretoria to immediately open all its places of detention to regular independent observers. Other international developments since the conference include resolutions condemning the detention of children by the European Economic Community in November; by the British House of Commons; by the United States' Senate in October; by the United Nations'

General Assembly in December.

However, there is no room for self-congratulation, no cause to relax the campaign to end South Africa's 'war on children'. It is clear from press reports that children are still in detention, still being detained, still enduring violence at the hands of the police and army. For example, within a week of the conference, two 14-year-old Bonteheuwel children were detained together with several other 15- and 16-year-olds. The children were released nearly a month later without charges, at about the same time that a 101-year-old man, Simon Mnquni, and three more 15-year-olds were detained in the Kwandebele bantustan. In Natal there have been many children among the over 150 fatalities in the conflict between Inkatha vigilantes and anti-apartheid youth, trade union and UDF activists. In other areas, children have recently died at the hands of Municipal Police and 'kitskonstabels' or police auxiliaries. On 17 December it was reported that members of the 'security forces' had raided a house in Tembisa shooting a 2-year-old and a 14-year-old. Another 14-year-old was shot dead after a 'stoning' incident in Beaufort West on 1 January.(The events cited within this paragraph were reported in the South African press, namely: *South* 12.11.87; *Sowetan* 27.11.87; *New Nation* 17.12.87 and *Cape Times* 5.1.88.)

Lawyers in South Africa report that while the scale of child detentions has diminished since the conference, the number being charged for activites relating to political protest has increased. In this way the number of official child detainees is kept low but the same children may spend several months in custody as awaiting-trial prisoners. If past statistics are anything to go by, most of these will be released shortly before any trial takes place, but only after the experience of several months in prison. Those eventually convicted face harsh sentences, in many cases entirely inappropriate for a child, or to the offence. For example, even though the magistrate noted that no-one had been killed or injured in the incidents, recently a 17-year-old was sentenced to 19 years' imprisonment for public violence, arson and attempted murder of a policeman in Sebokeng in 1986.

On 24 February 1988 the South African Government promulgated new emergency regulations which sought to restrict the popular anti-apartheid organisations. Seventeen of them were effectively prevented from carrying out any activities without government consent. Amongst them were the Detainees' Parents Support Committee and the Detainees' Support Committee, both of which had participated at the Harare Conference. Both had been prominent in monitoring the application of the emergency

123

Those who have to live with apartheid inside South Africa or in its shadow in the Front Line States know that the Commonwealth has been by their side, standing full square against a system which is the denial of all the Commonwealth represents. The mission of the Eminent Persons' Group last year tried hard to explore with South Africa and with South Africans black and white, coloured and Indian, the path to peaceful change. That helping hand was brushed aside because President Botha was not prepared to contemplate the journey to justice and to life.

Since then the Commonwealth has been in the forefront of the international movement for sanctions against South Africa, sanctions designed to compel the South African government to recognise that the time has come to change.

There are some in the world who in pointing to other abuses of human rights ask what is so special about South Africa. Our reply has been that it has been the grossest contemporary denial of our common humanity and a repudiation of our oneness as human beings. Apartheid in crystallising the evils which have scarred civilisation over the ages into a vile creed of racial supremacy is the modern face of slavery. It calls forth the same moral repugnance, the same guilt by association taints all who support and sustain it. It evokes the same rebellion in defence of human values.

But if the doubter needs any further evidence of the special evil that stains the subcontinent, let them see what has been revealed to you over these last few days.

From the Commonwealth Secretary-General His Excellency Mr Shridath Ramphal, who was unable to attend the conference but sent a message

I'm still shocked and impressed by what the children have told us about the horrible things police in South Africa did to them. I admire their tremendous courage in coming here and telling us all the things that have happened to them. I listened very carefully.

I am myself a police commissioner in Holland, in The Hague, in charge of the care of juvenile delinquents and in general, young people in trouble. Every time I told a South African here that I am a policewoman, they were startled at first. But immediately thereafter they would welcome me warmly.

I feel deeply ashamed that there are police who commit such atrocious acts. At the same time I consider it a great privilege that I can be here as a private person, which was made possible by the

124

local government and the Chief of Police in The Hague. As a commissioner of police, I say that it is utterly and totally absurd that black children are arrested arbitrarily and systematically before they have done anything at all, that their parents are not informed about it and are left in anxiety, that they are beaten, ill-treated, electrically-shocked, sexually abused, detained together with grown-ups and even killed.

There is not a single point of comparison between the law enforcement system in South Africa and that in my own country. In South Africa the police are the enemy, in Holland the police are there to protect you. In South Africa the police serve the white regime, in Holland the police serve law and justice, also with regard to individual people in authority up to the Prime Minister if he is violating the law.

In South Africa discrimination is the fundamental law, in our country discrimination is a punishable offence. In South Africa black children look at the police as an instrument of an illegitimate regime, with us the police are often seen by young people as protectors against ill-treatment by parents or other grown-ups. If they have done something wrong, they are often more afraid of the parents than of the police. In short, what the police in South Africa do to black children has absolutely no relation to my work as a commissioner of police, and it has absolutely nothing to do with law and justice in a democracy.

That is why I for one, could not and would not work with the police in present-day South Africa. For my part, the South African police in the service of such an illegitimate regime, should not be allowed to take part in or be members of any international police organisation.

Anneke Visser, Police Commissioner in the Netherlands, with responsibility for young people in trouble

laws and protesting against their imposition. Other organisations represented at Harare were similarly restricted, notably the United Democratic Front, the largest grouping of anti-apartheid organisations inside the country. In a separate measure the Congress of South African Trade Unions, the largest non-racial federation of black trade unions was ordered to refrain from political activity, including criticism of the emergency regulations or campaigning for the release of detainees.

The developments in South Africa since the conference should remind us that on the one hand the campaign against the apartheid government has had some effect, but that on the other hand the necessity for increased pressure is as urgent as ever.

Reflections on the Conference

Reverend Beyers Naude of the Dutch Reformed Church. He was silenced by the regime for seven years from 1977 under a banning order which prevented him from being quoted or even from preaching. A year after the ban was lifted he became General Secretary of the South African Council of Churches, a position he held for two years until 1987.

One evening at the conference he spoke while the participants were eating in a hall at the conference centre. Although whites had refused for decades to hear his witness against apartheid, those who had come from South Africa to the conference received him as one of their leaders

There is so much to say, the heart is so full of so many emotions, of joy on the one hand, of being together here in a way in which we never dreamed would have been possible. When this idea was first mentioned and mooted I said to those who approached us in the SACC, only a miracle will make it possible for us to possibly bring 30 to 60 people from South Africa to such a conference. The miracle has happened. After it became known that there would be such a conference we could have added at least two, three, four hundred names of people in South Africa who are more than eager to be here. And that in itself is to my mind already a clear indication of the deep feelings of commitment on the part of our community of South Africa to the whole struggle for liberation in which they say we want to be identified, we want to be there, we want to participate, we want to share, and we want to take back to our country what we know we have to do. And such a spirit is unconquerable. No action of the state, however repressive, however brutal it may be, can ever in any way conquer that spirit.

This morning there was, as some of you may have heard, a press statement of protest from the Minister of Law and Order of South Africa about this conference, and the impression given of so many people in detention, of so many forms of torture. I have to respond.

The first thing is that we are talking about what has been happening in South Africa in the last two or three years and I challenge the South African government to prove that any of the information that has been supplied by the responsible bodies with regard to statistics and figures and the suffering and the torture of the people, is incorrect or false. The Minister says that at present no child under the age of 15 is detained under the emergency regulations. He says there are only 3 young people aged 15 in detention, 28 16-year-olds, 84 17-year-olds: a total of only 115 under 18 years in detention. But there should not be one.

Time and again we are being indicted and we are being accused both inside South Africa and outside that we are the betrayers of the country, we are the people who are always busy accusing the country, maligning the country, we are non-patriotic, we are subversive, we are instigators: the list is growing every day. But we are the true patriots, we are the true people who love our country and all its people because we stand for truth and we stand for freedom and we stand for true liberation of our country.

The basis on which the future of a country is built is not the government's kind of law and order which nobody is going to applaud, or is able in a meaningful way to implement. Law and order without justice is disorder, and any form of stability without the truth and the basis for that, becomes eventually anarchy and chaos. I believe that we have a right and we have a duty to say this regardless of whether it is being heard in our country. But we know it is being heard, because if the government is not so disturbed about what is happening here, it would not be necessary to have sent out such a letter or such a telegram as this. It is because the government is aware of the fact that the things that have been happening in the past three, four years have deeply disturbed all of us and the world is taking note. I'm saying this also for the sake of my Afrikaner people, even if they do not want to hear, even if they do not want to listen, even if they are not prepared to do what is right and what is just. What we're doing here is for the sake of the liberation of all of our people, black and white including the Afrikaner people, especially those who may still be unconvinced. And if they call me a traitor because of what I am saying and what I am doing, then let this be so. But I don't accept the fact that they call me a traitor because it is not true, though I understand why some of them may be saying this. I am saying to them, true patriotism, true love for your country, true loyalty, is doing what we are doing, is warning the world, is appealing to the world, to say for God's sake help us in South Africa to get rid once and for all of the evils of this system. That is the salvation of our country, that is the true liberation for all our people black and white.

I'm glad that at least there are some of our white community, including a small but growing number of young Afrikaners, who begin to understand the message, and who say we know that the government is leading us to national suicide, is leading us nowhere, and that some of them at least come forward and say, for God's sake help us, we can't help ourselves. What encourages me,

My husband Olaf Palme was awarded, posthumously, the Albert Einstein Peace Prize in the United States, and the Jawaharlal Nehru Peace Prize in India.

Our family has decided that the prize money will be used for children and young people in South Africa who are the victims of the apartheid system: children who have lost their parents, children and young people who have not been able to study because of the colour of their skin, children who have been wounded, and who suffer from the consequences of the violence we have heard about today.

A group of people in South Africa have come together to form a committee which will be called the 'Olaf Palme Children's Trust'. They will be part of the work for the children's future in South Africa.

So we will, all of us, who have been here in Harare, and who will return to our countries, bear a message which we can never forget and I keep asking: ' Who cannot take a stand?'

Lisbet Palme, of Sweden

and what surprises me, time and again, is the magnanimity and the sense of forgiveness and the willingness on the part of the black community to stretch out their hands to us who have been the ones causing so much suffering and anguish and pain. I hear them say, if you're sincere we are prepared to accept you. It is incredible. I've seen the suffering and every time I use this as an example to white people who say they are Christians, by saying, for God's sake, if you really want to have a definition of what it means to be a Christian, come and listen to our black brothers and sisters when they are talking about the willingness to accept you if you are sincere. That is the true definition of a Christian which they are portraying through their lives.

I know that in the hearts of some of us there is a measure of concern, uncertainty, fear, which is understandable as we return to South Africa. I think it is important that we voice these fears, that we say this to one another. I know that some of you may say to me, yes, Beyers, it is very easy for you to say this, for you've got a measure of international protection. They won't touch you, but they will touch us, those of us who are not so well known, those of us who have become the innocent victims of that kind of action. I know that. And it adds to my own anguish and my own pain. I hope that in some small way we are able to stand up when some of us may have to pay the cost and to say no, we are not going to allow it. But also to say to them, the sacrifice that you are doing,

128

the price that you are paying, you're paying on behalf of all of us. We wish we could have prevented that, but we salute you for it, we honour you for it, and we support you for it, and we would try to do whatever is possible.

I hope that nothing will happen, I pray that nothing will happen but if it does, then I feel that those of us who are here and those of us who go back to our respective countries should be led to an even deeper commitment. It will deepen and strengthen our conviction to stretch out our hands, to enter into the struggle deeper than ever before until that day when the whole of South Africa, the whole country and all its people, will be free.

Looking back on Harare

Ruth Mompati, member of the National Executive Committee of the ANC, talking about the conference a few weeks after it ended

Harare was a very wonderful experience – wonderful in many ways. It was a very moving experience, it was saddening, it enraged me, it made me want to go to South Africa, to walk there and just get my hands on the South African Police. It filled me with emotion and I cried about certain things. On the other hand it was an experience which actually lifted my spirits. I said to one of my friends that Harare took ten years off my age, when I came back I was ten years younger. The experience of talking with people who came from South Africa was wonderful, and discussing issues with them, listening to their views, listening to their analysis of the situation in South Africa and the solutions that they have come out with, some of which had worked beautifully, others had failed – all this was inspiring. And hearing how they had reorganised themselves and gone onto the offensive again was very moving.

One of my experiences in Harare was talking to mothers whose sons had been executed. I spent a lot of time with the mother of Benjamin Moloise. This was particularly significant for me because when three others were executed, I was the Chief Representative in London and we had been carrying out campaign after campaign for the commuting of the death sentence passed on these comrades. Mrs Moloise, after her son's execution, had come out so strong, so brave that I could not quite comprehend it. I couldn't understand that a woman whose child, whose son, had been killed in cold blood, was so brave. She was so proud of her son, the son who had been killed, who had been taken away from her. Speaking to this woman so that I could learn more of her feelings, her understanding and how she looks at our struggle

Nothing can stand in the way of the determination and love of those who wage struggle for justice and human dignity. No one can silence that which has once found freedom. Although my family obligations and the duties in the government in the People's Republic of Mozambique have made it impossible for me to be physically with you in this moment of our common struggle, I hope that with me, you'll be remembering the voice of Samora, the voice of Mabhida, Mandela, and Sisulu, the voice of all the mothers of freedom, equality, brotherhood and peace.

I would like to add my voice to that of all mankind in condemning the apartheid regime. The world has lately been witness to a terrifying display of brutality and repression by the racist police, who come down with all their repressive machinery upon the heads of innocent children.

The student revolt has been going on for more than a decade now. But the apartheid regime is still very far from making the slightest concession to youth demands. Its response to the legitimate claims of South African young people has been the bayonet, shooting, mass arrests and torture. In Mozambique we are sadly familiar with the murderous fury of the loathsome regime of apartheid and its brutality to men and women, young and the old.

Our children, too, suffered the racist regime's violence and they are the ones who are turned into the main victims by the aggression, through armed bandits that South Africa continues to send against us and against our country. Homoine and Manjacaze are telling examples of the wave of massacres and of the scores of deaths of people pursued by the bandits who sow slaughter and genocide on our people. Nothing is immune to the terrorist activities of the armed bandits. Hospital, schools, shops, railways, bridges and roads; men and women, survivors of the massacre go on to suffer, they collapse at watching the children going without food, clothing and without housing.

Just to mention the three provinces most affected by armed banditry – Tete, Zambezia and Sofala – out of 2,107 primary schools that were there in 1983, 1,372 have been closed down or destroyed through the effects of war.

On a national scale about half a million pupils can no longer attend classes, or do so under the most difficult conditions. The lack of schooling for these thousands of children is compounded by the break-up of the family, and of precisely that social fabric which should offer them security, stability and affection. Their parents are either mad, wandering from place to place, fleeing from the armed bandits to escape violence or have been murdered.

The extended family cannot function since there is no family any more. It has been decimated by South African-backed actions. Even the children are put to the slaughter or brutalised or maimed. They see their mothers being raped, they see their fathers being murdered, their brothers and sisters being burnt alive, they are present at those ghastly scenes when an armed bandit takes the pounding stick to beat out the brains and heads of one of their friends.

From 1980 to 1985 the war was directly or indirectly responsible for the death of some 85,000 children per year in Mozambique. One child dies every four minutes in my country, as an apartheid victim.

The number of victims of terror and violence rises day by day and day by day more children present symptoms of mental and emotional disorder that will place a burden on our society for generations to come. This too is apartheid's crime that we must condemn and take action against.

For all these reasons we in Mozambique cannot be insensitive to discussions at this conference. We should like you to understand how deeply we identify with you and your cause. Our country cannot be truly free until apartheid is no more in South Africa, until the shadow of violence, the actors of massacres, the murderers, the injustice and the causes are eradicated from the face of our continent, until the moment when our children can smile and call 'daddy' to everybody in peace.

Graça Machel, in a message to the conference.

---

taught me a lot. So I spent a lot of time with her, talked to her and I was able to get to understand her way of thinking.

In fact she, like many of us, looks upon every young man of South Africa as her son. For her the loss of one son, one young South African youth, is the loss of her own son, and the saving of one South African young man is the saving of her son. The reason she felt she could not mourn her son was because of the strength that she had been given by the young man himself. She said, 'this is not my strength, this is the strength which I was given by my son, who said to me "Mother, it is all right, this is what I expected, this is what I was struggling for and this is the price that we must pay for our own liberation. My death – my murder by the South African regime – will mean the freedom of my own brothers and sisters, of my nation and my people".' She says that this was what gave her so much strength, seeing this son of hers just not afraid.

131

This gave me also very great strength. I felt that I had begun to understand. I had always thought that I understood and always considered the youth as my own children. But it is one thing when they are alive around you. It is another when you, as a mother, lose your son. She made me understand myself better and extended my understanding of the struggle, brought it home more vividly, more clearly and more realistically. She brought the reality of the sacrifices of the black mother more clearly to me.

I also met other mothers in Harare, wives of men who are on Robben Island and who have been in prison for the last 23 years. They are the colleagues of Comrade Nelson Mandela, the Rivonia Trialists. Their wives were there. I was very struck by these people. They are not sad or worried or pensive – in pensive mood. On the contrary, they are full of life, involved in what is happening in the country. Their role is in giving courage to young wives and young mothers whose husbands have just been arrested or whose husbands have just been killed. They themselves are a tower of strength and it gave me a very great feeling that here are people who have hardly seen their husbands for over 23 years and yet they are so strong, so full of ideas of what should be done in the struggle of the people of South Africa to win freedom.

And the youth and children at Harare also brought me a new understanding of their reality. Before 1976 our children of course lived under the brutality of the apartheid regime. They were old, although they were young, they had lost their childhood. But they lost it in a different way from in the present period, in that the brutalisation, then, by the apartheid regime, the malnutrition, the hunger, living under fear of the police all the time, had robbed them of the freshness of life, the young life that has no cares.

But 1976 heralded the new assault on the children of South Africa. For the first time the South African regime pointed their guns at our children and shot them in cold blood. For the first time our children got to know that when they see a policeman with a gun, that gun was no longer just meant for their parents, but it was meant for them too. This brought a change in the perspectives and the realities of the present life of our children, because they began to realise that they were no longer children, they could no longer behave as children, play, and do what children do. They had now become people who must defend themselves, not against beatings by the police, but against shootings by the police. Children began to think differently, began to think about how to become a soldier of Umkhonto we Sizwe. How can I learn to shoot? How do I become a defender of the people of South Africa? How do I become a member of the armed struggle. So they grew up not

132

wanting to play like children, not wanting to go to school like children, but wanting to go and to train as soldiers.

For instance, this is the kind of experience I've had with young people. A boy of 15 who came out from South Africa was told by our people to go to school, but refused point blank. So I went to this boy in a group of young men where he was the youngest, and I said 'What have you come here for?' He replied, 'Oh, we've come, we are going to train. We want to go and train.' So I said 'Don't be ridiculous, you are only children, you are 15. You must go to school.' And one of them said, 'Granny, please, we have come to train.' I said, 'No, you are too young to train, you must go to school and when you have finished your schooling, then you can come and train.' And the youngest said to me: 'Granny, we have come from South Africa to come and train. If we wanted to go to school, we would have stayed at home and studied. We came out because there is no possibility of us remaining in school and being safe. We have no way of defending ourselves against the police guns which attack us in the schools, and that is why we have left our country to come and train and that's what we want to do. And we want you to understand that we are not children, as you think, we are grown-ups. There are no children in South Africa. We have come to train, we want you to understand this.'

I looked at them and I realised that this young man was right, they were not children. Their way of talking, their way of thinking was not that of children. There was no way I could treat them as children and send them where I wanted them to go. There was only one thing to do, to discuss with them and understand what they wanted. So I said, 'All right, we'll talk, and if you insist on going to training, I don't think that I can insist on sending you to school, but I want you to remember that no matter how you feel, you are very young.' They said, 'No, granny, we know we are young, but we are not too young to go and defend ourselves.'

Even when the President spoke to them they wouldn't change their minds. They said, 'No, we want to go and train.' But suddenly you can see the child come through. After they had spoken to the President, refused to go to school, wanted to go and train, this young man then turns to the President and says: 'Grandfather, please bring me sweets, buy me sweets.' Deep down there is a child, but a child who has been made to forget childhood. Their childhood has been completely destroyed and this child now looks at things which a child should not be looking at, thinks of solutions to problems which he should not even know about.

So these are not children. South Africa has robbed our children

This conference is taking place at a very critical time in the struggle for national liberation in Namibia and South Africa. Our two peoples are fighting in order to create conditions that would be conducive to the care, protection and peaceful development of children, so that they may grow and reach adulthood.

Under the present political circumstances, the children of Namibia and South Africa are under constant threat and normal development is impossible for them now.

Many children are made orphans because their parents are killed. Their parents are also jailed, disappearing and deported to 'homelands' where they have no possibility of employment to support their families. In Namibia barbaric acts are daily carried out under the pretext of fighting Swapo and its military wing Plan. The racist army of occupation destroys schools, hospitals and clinics, leaving Namibian black children without primary health care and educational facilities.

These are just a few examples of the barbaric acts in Namibia carried out by South African army of occupation against children.

- In March this year an incident took place when fascist troops clashed with Swapo guerrillas. It was reported at the time that two Casspir military troop carriers retreating from the scene of fighting drove towards nearby black homes with their guns blazing in all directions. A small school girl sitting in a millet field eating her lunch was shot and killed instantly in the firing.

- A young boy Leonard Haikali was roasted alive in Northern Namibia by white soldiers. Speaking from his hospital bed where he was recovering and getting treatment for the burns he sustained, he said, 'The white soldier ordered a black soldier to make fire, then the white soldier ordered me to sit down on the fire, but I refused. He grabbed me and forcibly threw me into the flames. As I struggled he would kick me back in the flames'. Haikali sustained third-degree burns on his back, and those involved were never brought before a court of law.

- A school girl Mariam Kanyama was assaulted by white soldiers, had her arm broken and sustained head injuries. She was questioned about the whereabouts of Swapo guerrillas. When she replied that she knew nothing, she was grabbed by her arm, beaten with a branch of a tree, slapped across her face.

- In January this year a 14-year-old girl Christofina Thomas suffered serious injuries to her hip bones when she refused sexual intercourse with a white soldier. The girl has since undergone three operations, but she is still experiencing terrible pains in her lower abdomen.

- In June this year a 15-year-old school boy Portas Blasius sustained severe facial burns when members of the fascist South African army in Namibia forced his face against the exhaust pipe of an army truck. Speaking from his hospital bed, Portas said that he suffered at the hands of 'merciless white devils'. He was first taken to an unknown place and questioned about movements of Swapo guerrillas. They pulled his hair and forced his face against the exhaust pipe of a truck. He has suffered irreparable facial deformity.
- More than 13 black school complexes were burned down in Namibia during the past three months.

Like their counterparts in South Africa, Namibian children have never known a happy and secure childhood.

Dr Nickey Iyambo, representative of Swapo of Namibia

---

of their childhood, they have robbed us of the joy of bringing up young children, as our children are not young, they are old young people.

The children who came to Harare to tell of the things they do inside the country, their confrontation with the police, the work of the struggle which they carry out inside the country, speak of unbelievable experiences. It's a new education for you that children of this age are able to do these things. Except of course that we have learned similar lessons through the experiences of our friends. For instance, in Angola we learnt that children had played a very important role in the struggle for Luanda and the defeat of the South Africans and Unita. And today it is very encouraging and moving too, that these people do not feel that our presence there is a danger to them. On the contrary, they feel that ours is their struggle, that when they gained their independence they had not yet won the struggle for the liberation of Angola. They had not yet won liberation of their countries – front line countries. To have young people with that understanding is amazing, but this is the reality where there is struggle for true liberation, for true democracy and for peace.

Our children in South Africa have learned another political lesson too. The children have come to realise that if you act as individuals you get caught, you get shot and you can't win. They have come therefore to respect organisation. It has been through the community organisation that they have gained some kind of

135

If you look at my age, and the age in which I was born, you can clearly see that I'm a revolutionary child. I was born in a revolution and even today I'm still involved in the revolution, so you could say I was actually supposed to enter the fight.

Buras Nhlabathi a student at the ANC's Solomon Mahlangu Freedom College, and one of those who gave testimony at the Harare Conference

---

freedom from fear, from the fear that they used to have before. They feel they belong to an organisation which is fighting against apartheid and this gives them the strength of unity, the strength of collectivity, the strength of working together with others and of not being mere individuals, of not being alone. They understand the word 'comrade' because they see it actually working. They know you rely on your comrades, you depend on your collective, you depend on your organisation, knowing that your organisation will not let you down. The children know that they can only succeed if they are united in their action. Unity in action is what the ANC has called for, and unity in action is what our young people are implementing inside the country.

APPENDICES

APPENDIX I – CONFERENCE DECLARATION

The International Conference on Children, Repression and the Law in Apartheid South Africa, convened by the Rt. Reverend Archbishop Trevor Huddleston, CR, under the auspices of the Bishop Ambrose Reeves Trust, took place in Harare, Zimbabwe, from 24-27 September 1987. The opening session of the conference was addressed by the Hon Robert Mugabe, the Prime Minister of Zimbabwe, the President of the African National Congress, Oliver Tambo and Mrs Lisbet Palme of Sweden.

Almost 300 South Africans, the majority of whom had come from inside the country, met with over 200 representatives of more than 150 organisations from all over the world. There were lawyers, medical practitioners, religious and social workers, community and political activists and representatives of youth, student, and women's organisations as well as trade union and professional bodies. The delegation from inside the country included children, along with those whose work and experience bring them most directly into contact with the effects of the apartheid regime's brutal repression of children.

By bringing us together in Harare, the conference provided the international community with a unique opportunity to hear from those directly affected, the truth about the violent repression inflicted by apartheid, including the beating, shooting, torture, detention and imprisonment of children. It enabled us and the whole international community to break through the veil of censorship and secrecy imposed by the apartheid regime's two-year-old State of Emergency.

We heard moving testimony from children about their harrowing experiences of torture and injury at the hands of the regime's agents. Doctors and other professional workers concerned with the welfare of children, informed us about the reality of how children are treated under apartheid. Lawyers explained the absence of any effective legal provisions for the protection of children and their vulnerability in the face of the apartheid regime's determination to maintain the oppression of the majority of South Africans.

The cruelty and brutality which were exposed induced a profound sense of shock, outrage and anger. The deliberate and systematic targetting of children by the armed agents of the regime puts apartheid South Africa beyond the pale of civilised society. It exposes the political and moral bankruptcy of a system bent on

138

destroying any form of opposition. Such a form of government is totally illegitimate.

We strongly condemn all those who collaborate with the regime in executing its policies, in particular the lawyers and judges who lend legitimacy to an inhuman and illegitimate system and the medical practitioners who conspire in keeping secret the brutality against children. We call upon the international community to sever all relations with professional bodies which fail to condemn these practices.

We commit ourselves to act in a concerted way to keep the world aware of the plight of South Africa's children. We will continue, and extend, the task of monitoring and exposing the repression and abuse of children.

We urge lawyers, medical practitioners, social and religious workers, and all others whose work involves special responsibilities for children, to play a part in the struggle to protect the children of South Africa and help free them from apartheid.

We appeal to the international community to work for the imposition of sanctions against the regime, and urge all governments to declare their support for all those who, even at risk to themselves, are prepared to act in defence of the children of South Africa.

We recognise that the children of South Africa cannot lead a normal life as long as the apartheid system remains. The children themselves, having recognised this fact, have displayed heroic courage in their readiness to engage their ruthless oppressors in daily struggle. Their commitment and determination is an inspiration to us all. We pledge ourselves, collectively and as individuals, to use all our resources to work towards the realisation of a united, non-racial and democratic South Africa and thereby ensure a speedy end of the racial tyranny whose violence spares neither old nor young – in South Africa, Namibia and throughout Southern Africa.

APPENDIX II – INTERNATIONAL LAW AND THE CHILD.

Below is detailed information about the UN Declaration of the Rights of the Child, with comments by Richard Falk, and the text of Article 19 of the Draft Convention on the Rights of the Child.

United Nations Declaration of the Rights of the Child

The text of the Declaration is divided up into ten Principles that depict guidelines for preferential treatment. The assumption is that the child must be protected against societal deficiencies. Thus in Principle 8:

> The child shall in all circumstances be among the first to receive protection and relief.

And Principle 9:

> The child shall be protected against all forms of neglect, cruelty, and exploitation. He shall not be the subject of traffic, in any form.
> The child shall not be admitted to employment before an appropriate age.

Manifestly, the general operation of apartheid is an affront to these Principles, guidelines that are declaratory of obligations.

But Principle 10 addresses the overall abuse of children in the South African setting much more directly, even if not explicitly:

> The child shall be protected from practices which may foster racial, religious and any other form of discrimination. He shall be brought up in a spirit of understanding and tolerance, friendship among peoples, peace and universal brotherhood, and in full consciousness that his energy and talents should be devoted to the service of his fellow men.

Obviously, many states fall far short of these standards, but South Africa has legalised a system of rule that denies even the formal legitimacy of such aspirations on behalf of children. The welfare of children is also the explicit concern of Articles 23 and 24 of the International Covenant on Civil and Political Rights:

Article 23

1. The family is the natural and fundamental group unit of society and is entitled to protection by society and the State.
2. The right of men and women of marriageable age to marry and to found a family shall be recognised.
3. No marriage shall be entered into without the free and full consent of the intending spouses.
4. State Parties to the present Covenant shall take appropriate steps to ensure equality of rights and responsibility of spouses as to marriage, during marriage and at its dissolution. In the case of dissolution, provision shall be made for the necessary protection of any children.

Article 24

1. Every child shall have, without any discrimination as to race, colour, sex, language, religion, national or social origin, property or birth, the right to such measures of protection as are required by his status as a minor, on the part of his family, society and the State.
2. Every child shall be registered immediately after birth and shall have a name.
3. Every child has the right to acquire a nationality.

Article 10 of the International Covenant on Economic, Social and Cultural rights is also relevant:

Article 10

The States Parties to the present Covenant recognise that:

1. The widest possible protection and assistance should be accorded to the family, which is the natural and fundamental group unit of society, particularly for its establishment and while it is reponsible for the care and education of dependent children. Marriage must be entered into with the free consent of the intending spouses.
2. Special protection should be accorded to mothers during a reasonable period before and after childbirth. During such period working mothers should be accorded paid leave or leave with adequate social security benefits.
3. Special measures of protection and assistance

141

should be taken on behalf of all children and young persons without any discrimination for reasons of parentage or other conditions. Children and young persons should be protected from economic and social exploitation. Their employment in work harmful to their morals or health or dangerous to life or likely to hamper their normal development should be punishable by law. States should also set age limits below which the paid employment of child labour should be prohibited and punishable by law.

Article 19 of the Draft Convention on the Rights of the Child

The text of the provision:

1. States Parties to the present Convention recognise the right of children who are accused or recognised as having infringed the penal law to be treated in a manner which is consistent with promoting their sense of dignity and worth and intensifying their respect for the human rights and fundamental freedoms of others, and which takes into account their age and the desirability of promoting their rehabilitation.

2. To this end, and having regard to the relevant provisions of international instruments, the States Parties to the present Convention shall, in particular, ensure that:

(a) no child is arbitrarily detained or imprisoned or subjected to torture, cruel, inhuman or degrading treatment or punishment,

(b) capital punishment or life imprisonment without possibility of release is not imposed for crimes committed by persons below 18 years of age,

(c) children accused of infringing the penal law

(i) are presumed innocent until proven guilty according to law,

(ii) are informed promptly of the charges against them and, as of the time of being accused, have legal or other appropriate assistance in the preparation and presentation of their defence,

(iii) have the matter determined according to law in a fair hearing within a reasonable period of time by an independent and impartial tribunal and

(iv) if found guilty are entitled to have their conviction

and sentence reviewed by a higher tribunal according to law.

3. An essential aim of treatment of children found guilty of infringing the penal law shall be their reformation and social rehabilitation. A variety of dispositions, including programmes of education and vocational training and alternatives to institutional care, shall be available to ensure that children are dealt with in a manner appropriate and proportionate both to their circumstances and the offence.

4. All children deprived of their liberty shall be treated with humanity and respect for the inherent dignity of the human person, and shall in particular:

(a) be brought as speedily as possible for adjudication,
(b) be separated from adults accused or convicted of having committed an offence unless it is considered in the child's best interest not to do so, or it is unnecessary for the protection of the child, and
(c) have the right to maintain contact with their family through correspondence and visits, save in exceptional circumstances.

Harare Conference Documentation

GENERAL CONFERENCE WORKING PAPER

Apartheid's violence against children (*reprinted by IDAF – see below under 'Other Sources'*)

BACKGROUND DOCUMENTS

Rights of children under international law, Kader Asmal, University of Dublin, September 1987.

The State of Emergency law with special reference to the detention of children, N Haysom, August 1987, Centre for Applied Legal Studies,Johannesburg.

Torture and assault in detention, Detainees' Parents Support Committee press conference, 25 August 1987.

Juvenile political prisoners in South Africa and the deaths of juveniles in police custody, International Defence and Aid Fund for Southern Africa, September 1987.

Children and the law in South Africa: the child in the dock, D.J. McQuoid, University of Natal, September 1987.

South African security laws versus the child, Pius Langa, Spetember 1987.

Education as a liberatory force, Eric Molobi, National Education Crisis Committee, September 1987.

Psycho-social effects of exile on children, Zonke Majodina, September 1987.

Other Sources

Abantwana bazabalaza: a memorandum on children under repression, 1986, Catholic Institute for International Relations, London.

Apartheid's onslaught on the health of children, Elmiger, P.M., 1980, World Health Organisation (WHO), Geneva.

Apartheid's violence against children, Fact Paper on Southern Africa No.16, International Defence and Aid Fund, 1988, London.

Chairman of Special Committee Against Apartheid calls for action against detention of children in South Africa, 1980, United Nations, New York.

Children and detention, 'Free the Children' Alliance, June 1987, Johannesburg.

Children in places of detention, *South African Medical Journal*, June 1987.

Child is not dead,The: youth resistance in South Africa 1976-86, Harries, Ann (comp.) *et al.*, 1986, British Defence and Aid Fund for Southern Africa, London.

Child labour in South Africa: a general review, 1983, Anti-Slavery Society, London.

Children in crisis ; Children in need, 1986, Pietermaritzburg Agency for Christian Social Awareness, Pietermaritzburg.

Children in political trials in South Africa: evidence prepared by IDAF and submitted to the Ad Hoc Working Group of Experts established by the UN Commission on Human Rights, London, June 1980.

Children in prison in South Africa: a study commissioned by Defence for Children International, McLachlan, Fiona ; Van Zyl Smit, Dirk, 1984, University of Cape Town, Institute of Criminology, Cape Town.

Children on the frontline: the impact of apartheid, destabilization and warfare on children in Southern and South Africa, 1987, United Nations Children's Fund (UNICEF), New York.

Children: their courts and institutions in South Africa, McLachlan, Fiona, 1986, University of Cape Town, Institute of Criminology, Cape Town.

Children under apartheid, 1980, January, IDAF, London.

Children under apartheid, 1986, Defence of Children International, New York.

Focus on political repression, International Defence and Aid Fund for Southern Africa, London.

57 days in the life of Fanie Guduka, Learn and Teach, No. 1, 1986, Johannesburg.

Growing up in a divided society: the contexts of childhood in South Africa, Burman, Sandra and Reynolds, Pamela (eds.), 1986, Ravan Press, Johannesburg.

Health of children in South Africa, The: some food for thought, Moosa, A., *The Lancet*, 7 April 1984.

Last affidavits, The: [collected by Brian Bishop and Molly Blackburn in Bhongolethu township, Oudtshoorn], 1987, Southern African Catholic Bishops' Conference, Johannesburg.

Memorandum on the detention of children, 1986, Committee of Concern for Children, Johannesburg.

Memorandum on the suffering of children in South Africa, 1986, Black Sash, Johannesburg.

Never on your knees : youth in apartheid South Africa, Strachan, Brigid, 1985, United Nations Association Youth (UNA), London.

Police conduct during township protests, August-November 1984, Report on:, November 1984, South African Catholic Bishops Conference, London.

Punishment by process, Sash, May 1987.

Repression and violence against children and young people by the apartheid regime: a selection of reports, affidavits and statements . . . 1986, International Defence and Aid Fund, London.

Role of the police and other arms of the state in recent strikes and demonstrations in South Africa, 1980, UN Commission on Human Rights, United Nations, New York.

Survey of Race Relations in South Africa, Annual:, South African Institute of Race Relations, Johannesburg.

Two dogs and freedom: children of the townships speak out, 1986, Ravan Press/Open School, Johannesburg.

War against children, The: South Africa's youngest victims, 1986, Lawyers Committee for Human Rights, New York. (Updated December 1986)

Visits to prisons, May 1986, Saxe, Prof. Norma; Ellsworth, Dr Margaret.